OXFORD WORLD'S CLASSICS

BRITANNICUS, PHAEDRA, ATHALIAH

JEAN RACINE was born in December 1639 at La Ferté-Milon, about forty miles north-east of Paris. The family were well-established in the town, where his father and grandfather held minor official appointments. His mother died when he was two years old, his father when he was four, and he was brought up by his paternal grandparents. After his grandfather's death his grandmother retired to the convent of Port-Royal des Champs, and he was educated in the neighbourhood of the convent and at the college of Beauvais. He was a brilliant student, and acquired an exceptional knowledge of Greek and Latin literature, both classical and Christian. His early life was secluded, but before he was twenty he had already begun to mix with poets and theatrical people in Paris and became acquainted with, among others, La Fontaine and Molière. After a short period with an uncle at Uzès, where his family had sent him with a view to an ecclesiastical career, he returned to Paris and resumed his literary and theatrical acquaintance. In 1664 and 1665, he saw the production of his first two plays, *La Thébaïde* and *Alexandre le Grand*, by Molière's company, but he took the latter play to another company and broke with Molière. Thereafter his closest literary association was with Boileau. A series of major plays, including *Britannicus* (1669), fills the years from *Andromaque* (1667) to *Phèdre* (1676); this was the period of Racine's most fertile production and greatest success as a dramatist. There followed a gap of twelve years, in which he married, was appointed historiographer to Louis XIV, and turned his thoughts more attentively to religion. In 1689 and 1690 two further plays, *Esther* and what many have considered to be his greatest play, *Athalie*, were produced, but before restricted audiences only. They were on subjects from the Old Testament and had the patronage of Madame de Maintenon. The favour Racine enjoyed from Louis XIV was interrupted by a singular act of gaucherie on the part of the poet. He died in 1699.

C. H. SISSON was born in Bristol in 1914, and educated at local state schools and at the University of Bristol, with post-graduate studies in Paris and Berlin. *In the Trojan Ditch* (collected poems and selected translations) appeared in 1974, and later publications have included translations of Lucretius, Dante, Du Bellay, and Virgil, a version of *La Chanson de Roland* for Radio 3, and *Collected Poems 1943–83* (1984). He is married, with two daughters and four grandchildren, and lives in Somerset. He was made an Hon. D.Litt. by the University of Bristol in 1980.

OXFORD WORLD'S CLASSICS

*For over 100 years Oxford World's Classics have brought
readers closer to the world's great literature. Now with over 700
titles—from the 4,000-year-old myths of Mesopotamia to the
twentieth century's greatest novels—the series makes available
lesser-known as well as celebrated writing.*

*The pocket-sized hardbacks of the early years contained
introductions by Virginia Woolf, T. S. Eliot, Graham Greene,
and other literary figures which enriched the experience of reading.
Today the series is recognized for its fine scholarship and
reliability in texts that span world literature, drama and poetry,
religion, philosophy and politics. Each edition includes perceptive
commentary and essential background information to meet the
changing needs of readers.*

OXFORD WORLD'S CLASSICS

═══

JEAN RACINE

Britannicus
Phaedra
Athaliah

═══

Translated with an Introduction and Notes by
C. H. SISSON

OXFORD
UNIVERSITY PRESS

OXFORD
UNIVERSITY PRESS

Great Clarendon Street, Oxford OX2 6DP

Oxford University Press is a department of the University of Oxford.
It furthers the University's objective of excellence in research, scholarship,
and education by publishing worldwide in

Oxford New York

Athens Auckland Bangkok Bogotá Buenos Aires Calcutta
Cape Town Chennai Dar es Salaam Delhi Florence Hong Kong Istanbul
Karachi Kuala Lumpur Madrid Melbourne Mexico City Mumbai
Nairobi Paris São Paulo Shanghai Singapore Taipei Tokyo Toronto Warsaw
with associated companies in Berlin Ibadan

Oxford is a registered trade mark of Oxford University Press
in the UK and in certain other countries

Published in the United States
by Oxford University Press Inc., New York

Translation, Introduction, Note on the Text, Chronology,
and Explanatory Notes © C. H. Sisson 1987

The moral rights of the author have been asserted

Database right Oxford University Press (maker)

First published 1987 by Oxford University Press in the
World's Classics series and simultaneously in a hardback edition
Reissued as an Oxford World's Classics paperback 2001
Reissued 2009

British Library Cataloguing in Publication Data

Racine, Jean
Britannicus, Phaedra, Athaliah.
I. Title. II. Sisson, C. H. III. Racine,
Jean [Phèdre, English]. Phaedra. IV. Racine,
Jean [Athalie, English]. Athaliah.
842'.4 PQ1888.F5

Library of Congress Cataloging in Publication Data

Racine, Jean 1639–1699
Britannicus, Phaedra, Athaliah.
1. Racine, Jean, 1639–1699—Translations, English.
2. Britannicus, 41–55—Drama. 3. Phaedra (Greek
mythology)—Drama. 4. Athaliah, Queen of Judah—
Drama. I. Sisson, C. H. (Charles Hubert), 1914– .
II. Title: Britannicus. III Title: Phaedra.
IV. Title: Athaliah.
PQ1888.F5S56 1987 842'.4 86–19977

ISBN 978–0–19–955599–4

10

Printed and bound in Great Britain
by Clays Ltd, Elcograf S.p.A.

CONTENTS

ACKNOWLEDGEMENT

I SHOULD like to thank Roger Pearson of the
Queen's College, Oxford, for his acute and sensitive
comments on the translation. The final text has
benefited by his suggestions and the flaws remain
my own.

INTRODUCTION

We get a glimpse of the young Jean Racine in the letters he
wrote from Uzès, at the age of twenty. He had been sent there
in search of a career: it had to be either the Church or the law,
and he had an uncle in Uzès who was a canon. In Paris he had
already made himself known by an ode on the marriage of
Louis XIV (1660), and he had become acquainted with La
Fontaine and with Molière, who was seventeen years his senior
and already very fashionable; his family feared that he might
be getting into bad company, mixing with theatrical and
literary people. The account he gives La Fontaine of his journey
to the south is full of curiosity and enthusiasm. He enjoyed, on
the way to Lyons, the company of three Huguenots, an English-
man, two Italians, a lawyer from Paris, two officials, and two of
the royal musketeers, and was man of the world enough—or
mean enough—to ride ahead each day to make sure of his bed
before the others turned up. He continued the journey on the
Rhône, spending nights at Vienne and Valence. He remarks that
at Lyons he began 'hardly to understand the language . . . or to
be understandable' himself. At Valence indeed he asked for a
chamber-pot, and found that instead a warming-pan was put in
his bed. Further south, he says, he was as much in need of an
interpreter as a Muscovite would be in Paris. But he quickly discovered that Provençal was 'a mixture of Spanish and Italian',
and being a linguist of talent and already familiar with those
languages, he found his way well enough. He describes how he
encountered his first olive-trees, and was rash enough to pick
and eat some of the fruit; and 'God preserve me', he says, 'from
ever feeling such bitterness again'. He 'could not get the taste
out of his mouth for four hours afterwards', and discovered that
many 'ceremonies' had to be gone through before the olive was
fit to eat. And the women were so good-looking! There was 'not
a village-girl, not a laundress' who could not challenge the most
beautiful in Paris. All this did not put poetry out of his mind.
He missed his literary friends. 'Do not imagine', he says a few
months later, 'that there is any lack of poets in the provinces;
on the contrary, they are abundant, but these Muses are different

from the others.' The career his mind was on was not exactly the one his family had proposed. Anyhow, his uncle the canon did not in the end come up trumps; by 1663 Racine was back in Paris.

In spite of his diversions, the young poet was far from being a bad candidate for Holy Orders, as the career was then understood. Born in 1639 in La Ferté-Milon, about forty miles northeast of Paris in what has since become the department of the Aisne, he came from a modest and solid family of local officials, and the accidents of his growing up had thrown him into the midst of one of the most significant religious movements of his time, a movement to which Pascal also came by a very different route, and which centred on the convent of Port-Royal. Racine had lost his mother when he was two years old, his father when he was four, and he was brought up by his paternal grandparents. It was his grandmother, Marie Desmoulins, who exercised the decisive influence. In 1649, a few years after her husband's death, she withdrew to Port-Royal des Champs, and it is thought that she took her grandson with her. From the age of ten, therefore, he was not only in the shadow of the convent but, no doubt, under the tutelage of the devout and scholarly men who had withdrawn from the world to live as 'solitaries' in the immediate neighbourhood. For two years, 1653–5, he was sent away to the college of Beauvais, where the solitaries of Port-Royal had friends, but at the age of sixteen he was back again as one of the few distinguished pupils at the Petites Écoles. He was an accomplished student, one might say, scholar, and acquired a ready familiarity with the Greek and Latin classics and with the early literature of the Church. The young man who wrote to La Fontaine from Uzès could not be said to have been without preparation for the ecclesiastical living he was supposed to be looking for.

His career was in fact to be of a different kind. There is another glimpse of him in his late fifties, near the end of his life, in the brilliant memoirs of Saint-Simon. Recording his death in 1699, Saint-Simon gives a vivid account of an incident a couple of years earlier. By that time, he says, the poet was on such terms with Louis XIV that sometimes, when the king was in Madame de Maintenon's apartments and there were no ministers present, he would send for Racine to amuse them. This was, of course, at the epoch when Madame de Maintenon had become active in works of piety and had included the king in her reformation. 'Unfortunately', Saint-Simon says, 'Racine could be rather absent-minded.' One day, when Louis was asking why the theatre had so deteriorated, Racine so far forgot himself that, having said there were no longer any good playwrights, he added that the actors were now digging up such old rubbish as the plays of Scarron. The trouble was that Scarron had been Madame de Maintenon's husband. 'The poor widow blushed,' says Saint-Simon. 'The king was embarrassed, and the sudden silence made Racine wake up and realize that his fatal absent-mindedness had pitched him into a well. He was the most put out of the three, and dared not even raise his eyes or open his mouth.' The silence lasted for several moments. Then the king said he had work to do, and dismissed Racine from his presence. 'After that', Saint-Simon records, 'neither Madame de Maintenon nor the king ever spoke to Racine again, or even looked at him.' The court of Louis XIV was hardly the place for such inadvertence.

The career which had brought the unemployed young man of Uzès to this splendour, and to this fall, had included not only his work as a dramatist, which had ended several years before with two plays, Esther and Athalie (written under the auspices of Madame de Maintenon, already devout and not yet insulted by the poet), but employment as historiographer to the king, responsible with his friend Boileau for recording the king's exploits. His career had been a success and had brought him considerable wealth. It had not, however, been without its set-backs, and he is certainly not to be thought of as lording it over the literary world of his day. His early poems, written while he was still in the seclusion of Port-Royal des Champs, include verses on the rural landscape which show that he was not insensible to the charms of the place. When he came back from his brief stay in the south he renewed his acquaintance with Molière, and presumably lived more or less free of the restrictions his family had formerly imposed upon him. The outstanding tragic poet of the time was Corneille (1603–84), whose great days were already over, and if Racine looked first in that direction, it was not for long. He had his first great success with Alexandre le Grand (1665), which was played by Molière's company. It was the talk of Paris and the critical comparison of the two tragedians, which has echoed down the centuries and found its way into the examination-rooms, dates from those first productions. Racine, who in his twenties was no doubt more temperamental, and more ambitious, than he allowed himself to appear later on, suddenly took his piece away from Molière's company to the rival company at the Hôtel de Bourgogne. What effect this had on the development of Racine's work it is hard to say, but the help and advice he seems earlier to have had from Molière not unnaturally came to an end and he turned for literary advice not to the great comic dramatist but to Boileau. Boileau, a frank and severe critic and himself a master of language and versification, was no doubt, in his temperament and in his scholarly and religious interests, more akin to Racine than Molière was; and Racine, beginning to go his own way in a marked fashion, may have found a man three years his junior more tolerable than the famous comic writer so much his senior. Racine at this time was certainly much concerned with his future as a literary man. When Nicole, one of the important figures of Port-Royal, spoke slightingly of playwriting as a not very honourable profession, and 'horrible when considered in the light of Christian principles', Racine weighed into him mercilessly with a brief and brilliant tract of his own. He had clearly moved away from his early religious masters.

Racine's career as a dramatist, after this time, consists of two unequal and widely separated parts. The first, beginning with Andromaque in 1667, ended a little more than a decade later with Phèdre (1676). It was the period of Racine's most fertile production and, allowing for a few ups and downs, of public success. In a dozen years he had written and seen played eight or nine major pieces, including Britannicus, Bérénice, Iphigénie, and finally Phèdre. Then followed a gap. Racine married, and thereafter his time and attention seem largely to have been divided between his family and the court. It was in 1677 that he was appointed historiographer to the king. One cannot say that Racine withdrew from the world, but he withdrew from whatever he did not think it his duty to do. In terms of the most popular moralities of the twentieth century, this must seem to be rather scandalous behaviour. He became reconciled with his old masters at Port-Royal, and employed his considerable talents as a man of affairs on their behalf, particularly after his aunt, Agnès de Sainte-Thècle, became abbess in 1690. To all appearances, Racine's career as a dramatist was over. He had renounced tragedy, and would no doubt have persevered in this intention had not an appeal, one might almost say a command, come to him from an unlikely quarter. Madame de Maintenon who, since she spoke also for Louis XIV, was not to be resisted, asked him to write something for 'the ladies of the Community of Saint-Louis' at Saint-Cyr, 'for the edification and instruction of the young ladies committed to their care'. The result was *Esther*, a tragedy the subject of which was drawn from the Old Testament. The piece was acted by the girls at Saint-Cyr in 1689, and published soon afterwards. Madame de Sévigné said: 'Racine has surpassed himself; he loves God as he used to love his mistresses.' She knew enough of the world, and of religion, to mean what she said. *Athalie*, the last and it may be the greatest of Racine's tragedies, was played at Saint-Cyr at the beginning of 1691. It was 1721 before the piece was played in Paris by professional actors. Racine had died in 1699.

Of the three plays in this volume, the first was written at the age of thirty, the second at the age of thirty-seven, and the third, after the long silence, at the age of fifty-one. *Britannicus* takes a theme from Roman history; the subject of *Phaedra* is mythological; *Athaliah* is based on the historical books of the Old Testament. In all of them the plot is worked out in a masterly fashion, moving from point to point swiftly and with great economy of design. All show a profound knowledge of the human mind and motives; they are at once passionate and analytical, in a manner which makes most of the romantic and post-romantic work of our own time seem childish or at best adolescent. Yet there is a deep personal element in all of them. Racine certainly does not display the incidents and oddities of his own life, as so many lesser writers do, but he draws on the whole of his experience. His life, so far as we know it—and on the whole we know little of the lives of the older writers—can hardly be said to have been full of the sort of material beloved of literary biographers, but he knew, besides the world of the theatre, the solitary world of retreat and self-analysis and the great practical world of the most powerful political centre of his time, the court of Louis XIV. In all these milieux he had lived not as a mere observer but as a participant in their very different preoccupations and affairs. In each of them he had had his own ambitions, checks, and successes. There is nothing in him of the supercilious or knowing airs of those who pretend, almost always with a false show of frankness, merely to be reporting what they have seen; he is a human being before he is a writer; he has suffered as well as seen others suffer, enjoyed as well as watched others amusing themselves; he has had successes as well as failures, and he knows the limitations of both. To his acute sensitivity, his practical good sense, and his penetrating intelligence which enabled him to understand so much, he brought the highest literary accomplishments of an age which was not short of such accomplishments.

Britannicus was performed for the first time at the theatre of the Hôtel de Bourgogne on 13 December 1669. The reader can gather from Racine's first preface to the play what difficulties it encountered. There seems to have been an organized claque of literary operators—not an extinct phenomenon, in the different circumstances of our own time—whose business was to try to ensure that it did not succeed. Corneille, whose work was in a taste he had largely created and did not wish to see superseded, watched from a box and before leaving the theatre spread around what he hoped would be damaging criticisms. Naturally the critics spoke well of the actors, whom they might need themselves on another occasion. The theatre was somewhat less full than it might have been, for a reason which had nothing to do with literary intrigue. There was an execution in a square nearby and many people naturally preferred the real horrors of that event to the best of tragedies on the stage. The play seems to have run for a few evenings, but less than might have been expected; Racine's second preface, written six years after the first, shows that in due course the play lived down the criticisms. The predominant position of the court, in the France of the time, no doubt gave actuality to the world of imperial Rome; and comparisons were not, after all, to the discredit of the French court, while the habits of flatterers and the irruptions of personal ambition were seen to operate in much the same ways in both. The Nero of Racine's play is not yet the monster of cruelty and insanity his original became; Racine shows him at the moment, so to speak, when he gave up playing the game of virtue and showed his true character. The emperor's mother, Agrippina, already has a long history of crime behind her; she is shown at the point when her long-standing ambition to rule the empire is threatened and broken. Britannicus, whom her intrigues had deprived of the succession which might have been his, is an adolescent in love with a girl, Junia, brought up in seclusion; and he trusts his tutor Narcissus who has been put in place to betray his confidence and to ensure that he remains powerless. Virtue does not triumph; indeed the triumph of vice is resounding, with the poisoning of Britannicus and the escape of Junia to the Vestals, the nearest thing classical Rome knew to the convents which played so important a part in seventeenth-century France. The complexity of the relationships between the characters is immense, but not for a moment does Racine lose himself. The plot develops remorselessly to the dénouement. Nor does the intensity of the passions evoked ever deprive the language of its beautiful lucidity.

Despite the part played by the love of Britannicus and Junia in preparing the final disaster, the theme of *Britannicus* is rather ambition and the intrigues of political power than love. In *Phaedra* love—one might almost say the horrors of love—becomes central. The play was performed for the first time on 1 January 1677, either in Paris, at the Hôtel de Bourgogne, or at Versailles. Two days later another play on the same subject appeared. It was a negligible work by a man called Pradon, promoted apparently as part of an intrigue by influential persons, headed by the Duchess of Bouillon, whose notions of making and unmaking literary reputations had nothing to do with the merits of the work in question. This rivalry was enough to cast a blight on Racine's tragedy, although, as usual, the supposed masterpiece of the moment rapidly faded from sight. Literary intrigue accounts, however, for only part of the difficulties Racine encountered; he was broaching subjects which his contemporaries did not expect to see treated on the stage. Hippolytus was the son of Phaedra's husband, Theseus, by another connection, and her love was criminal. Racine, in developing his subject from Euripides, must have been well aware of the scandal he might cause; he is said to have maintained that 'a good poet could make people excuse the greatest crimes', and even 'inspire pity for their misfortunes'. Phaedra is, in fact, a striking and sympathetic figure, which is not to say that Racine was attempting to convert her vice into virtue, or that he regarded her crime with anything but horror. His analytical powers went deep and his capacious imagination refused nothing of the truth as he saw it, and horror did not preclude sympathy. The play is one of the most remarkable productions not merely of the French but of the whole European theatre, and its relative failure was a blow to Racine, although to suppose, as has sometimes been done, that this setback was the only or even the chief reason for the long silence which followed is to misunderstand the complexity of his mind and the many other elements in his situation. A subsidiary attraction of the play which will strike the reader of the twentieth century is the mythological background of the plot. Phaedra is 'the daughter of Minos and Pasiphaë', of the Cretan lawgiver and the princess who conceived a passion for a sacrificial bull—a union which produced the fabulous, half-human Minotaur. The death of Hippolytus, which was at the hands of another monster who came out of the sea at the bidding of Neptune, adds a further touch of mythological horror and evokes the mysterious Mediterranean world just beyond the fringes of history.

The third play in this volume, *Athaliah*, produced for the first time in the winter of 1690–1, evokes a very different but hardly less terrible world. It is extraordinary that a tragedy, so ruthless in its dénouement and so harsh in its representation of the historical scene, should have been introduced to the world by, one might say, schoolgirls in a highly sheltered establishment. There were a few performances, in the girls' ordinary clothes, at Saint-Cyr and later one or two at Versailles, in Madame de Maintenon's apartments. These restricted audiences, and these immature and inexperienced actors, were all the play had in the author's lifetime. So ended the career of France's greatest dramatist. *Athaliah*, the plot of which is as tightly drawn as those of the other two plays in this volume, like *Esther* borrows from Greek tragedy the device of a chorus—a device perhaps adopted in the first place to give more girls a part in the performance but, like everything Racine touched, turned to dramatic effect. The persons of the play, and the substance of the plot, are such as to call up all Racine's austerity of tone. The texture of the verse is like steel. Jehoiada, the high priest, speaks not only for the faithful remnant of Judah, in a world given over to the worship of Baal; it is impossible not to hear also the voice of the secluded and sometimes persecuted men and women of Port-Royal. It would be wrong to look for historical parallels which would give a personal flavour to Racine's prophetic vein; his work at once soars above and penetrates below contemporary events. But it is fair to say that, without the experience of Port-Royal, he would never have written *Athaliah*. Moreover, the story of Joash calls up all the force of the poet's own devotion to the race of Louis XIV. The young king of David's line, who himself does not know that he is the king, is brought up in the temple and finally, as the plot develops, produced as the person on whom all the hopes of Judah are centred. At the same time, the temple is threatened by the faithless queen Athaliah, so that the tension between the poet's loyalty and his devout hatred of unjust authority is acute. The Old Testament story is terrifyingly alive, and there is no temptation for the reader to dismiss these themes as belonging to irrelevant old times, either of Old Testament days or of Racine's own. The poet disengages from the accidents of the events the enduring movements of ambition, loyalty, cruelty, and vindictiveness, such as they appear in all times and places, under the changing disguises of the moment, and over all broods Racine's sense of the immanence and transcendence of the Divine.

One can understand how the Romantic movement, looking back over a couple of centuries in which classical—and primarily Latin—literature had held the centre of the stage, came to under-value such a master as Racine. Classical notions had been in use for so long that they provided only a superficial dress for literary invention. Hazlitt went so far as to say that 'there is scarcely one stroke of original genius, nor anything like imagination', in Racine's writings. That is rubbish, of course, but most literature since the early nineteenth century has been more or less romantic and the editor of the Pléiade edition of the poet, walled up himself in the conventions of our own time, does not get much further. Even Valéry hardly manages to emancipate himself from the prejudices of the twentieth century. The early Romantics were concerned with what they saw as the weaknesses common to all classical drama—the insistence on the unities of time and place, the lack of local colour, the limitations of a scrupulously limited vocabulary, a certain nobility of tone which is not in the manners of later times. Yet it is because Racine proceeds with such exquisite sureness along a route which the literature of recent times has half closed to us that he can be so illuminating. For us there is novelty on every page. We are not here confronted with a literature which is confessional, or which pretends to the sort of realism which loses itself in tedious detail. What we have instead is a mind of great lucidity moving with consummate skill among all the storms and earthquakes of passion but never losing its poise. One might almost say that, after the successive assaults of Romanticism and Realism, we have ceased to understand the nature of the poetic drama. Even in Shakespeare characters do not say what a real person would have said in the dramatic circumstances; they say what such a person would have said if he had been endowed with the gift of speech to the extent that Shakespeare was endowed with it. As Hamlet in effect told the players, it is the poet and not the actor who is to supply the modulations. In Racine the business of *representing* passion in speech, rather than pretending to report the speech of people in a passion, is not essentially different. The conventions of the theatres differ; the art is essentially the same. It is the poet who speaks to us through various masks, through the choice of language, through the movement of the verse.

It remains only to say a word about the translation. Nothing can adequately represent in English the movement of the French alexandrine, the rhymed couplets which are the classic French form, and the form used by Racine. To offer as an equivalent some crude version of English heroic couplets—in pentameters— as more than one modern translator has done, is frankly absurd. Even the classic couplets of the real performers in this field, of Dryden or of Pope, would not entirely fill the bill, though they would of course have been the best available form for those two poets, had either attempted a version. A poet-translator has always to start from the forms of his own time, as he has to start from his own language. No one who had written poems of his own would suppose that the choice could be other than intuitive. The form I have used is a development of English blank verse, based on an eleven-syllable rather than a ten-syllable line, and on four stresses rather than five, but allowing for a certain freedom in both characteristics. As to the language, a certain propriety of speech is necessary to convey any suggestion of the tone of the original, and if propriety is not a quality much sought after by writers of our day, that does not mean that it is not desirable.

NOTE ON THE TEXT

THE text of Racine's plays presents no major problems, and the reader who wishes to compare these translations with the original can do so in any of the editions ordinarily available. The best modern scholarly edition is that of Philip Butler (C.U.P., 1967).

The plays were published separately at the time of their first production. There were collected editions in 1676 and 1697. The latter was the last published in Racine's lifetime and of course the first to contain *Phèdre* (1677) and *Athalie* (1691) as well as *Britannicus* (1670). It is this text of 1697 that I have mainly followed, using the pre-war edition (N.D.) of D. Jouast, published by Flammarion in the Librairie des Bibliophiles. I have however also made use of the monumental edition of Paul Mesnard (1865–73), in the Grands Écrivains de France series, which remains a great source of Racine scholarship, and the Pléiade edition, edited by Raymond Picard, which like Jouast is based on the text of 1697 but, unlike the Jouast edition, has modernized spelling.

Britannicus: Apart from some dozen lines in which small verbal changes were made after the editions of 1670–6, there are two short passages apparently omitted by Racine after the first printing of 1670. One omission shortens by 8 lines a speech of Britannicus in Act V, Scene 1; the other is of 12 lines of dialogue between Nero and Junia between Scenes 5 and 6 of Act V. Neither is significant for the action of the tragedy.

Phèdre: The only difference in the text after 1677 are verbal changes in some half a dozen lines.

Athalie: An even smaller number of verbal changes was made after 1691.

A CHRONOLOGY OF
JEAN RACINE

1638 Birth of the future Louis XIV.

1639 Jean Racine is baptized on 22 December at Ferté-Milon (Aisne), where his father is an official concerned with the local collection of indirect taxes—a relatively minor office which has been in the family for several generations.

1641 A second child, Marie Racine, is baptized on 24 January; the mother (Jeanne Racine, née Sconin) dies and is buried on 29 January.

1642 The poet's father remarries on 4 November—Madeleine Vol, of whom little more is known—and dies three months later at the age of 27. Jean and Marie are brought up by their maternal grandfather, Pierre Sconin.

1643 Louis XIII dies. Louis XIV succeeds to the throne, with his mother as Regent.

1649 Racine begins his studies at the Petites Écoles de Port-Royal; his aunt and his paternal grandmother are at the convent.

1653–5 Racine continues his studies at the Collège de Beauvais, which has links with Port-Royal.

1658–9 Racine completes his studies at the Collège d'Harcourt in Paris. During this period he makes his first literary acquaintance, and takes an interest in the quarrels surrounding the Lettres provinciales in which Pascal, who had become closely associated with Port-Royal, attacks the Jesuits.

1661 Louis XIV takes over the reins of government.
Racine goes to stay with his uncle Sconin in Uzès, in the hope of being established in an ecclesiastical benefice. The prospects fade and he returns to Paris in January 1663.

1664 Racine's first play, La Thébaïde, followed by Alexandre le Grand (1665).

1666 Racine composes his Lettre à l'auteur des Imaginaires, which marks a break with his masters at Port-Royal.

1667 Andromaque, followed in 1668 by a comedy, Les Plaideurs.

1669 Britannicus is produced, and encounters some hostility from Corneille. The following years see a succession of tragedies, Bérénice (1670), Bajazet (1672), Mithridate (1673), Iphigénie (1674) and Phèdre (1677).

1677 Racine marries Catherine de Romanet, by whom he has seven children from 1678 to 1692. He is appointed historiographer to the King. He is reconciled with Port-Royal and has apparently abandoned his career as a dramatist.

1683 Louis XIV marries Madame de Maintenon.

1685 The Revocation of the Edict of Nantes, which has since 1598 guaranteed the liberties of Protestants. Louis XIV is now profoundly under the influence of Madame de Maintenon and of the Jesuit Père La Chaise.

1688 Madame de Maintenon asks Racine for an instructive piece, with no love in it, which could be played by the girls of Saint-Cyr. Racine complies, after some hesitation, and *Esther* is produced accordingly in January 1689.

1690 *Athalie* is completed, and is produced, in a muted manner, without costume or stage, before Louis XIV and Madame de Maintenon, in January 1691. The play had no public performances and made little impression when it appeared in print.

1695–9 Racine wrote the *Abrégé de l'histoire de Port-Royal*.

1699 Death of Racine.

1715 Death of Louis XIV.

BRITANNICUS

tragedy

1669

OF all the works I have given to the public, there is none which has attracted more praise, or more critics, than this one. Whatever care I took to polish this tragedy, it seems that the harder I tried to make it good, the more certain people tried to decry it. They formed every possible clique and thought of every possible criticism. They even took sides with Nero against me. They said that I made him too cruel. I thought the mere name of Nero meant something more than cruel. But perhaps they are refining on his history, and mean that he was a respectable character in his early years. It is necessary only to have read Tacitus to know that if for a time he was a good emperor, he was always a very bad man. It is not, in my tragedy, a question of outside affairs. Nero is here in private and with his family. And they will excuse me from recalling for them all the passages which could quite easily prove to them that I need not apologize to him.

Others, on the contrary, have said that I made him too good. I confess that I had not imagined a good man in the person of Nero. I have always regarded him as a monster. But here he is a budding monster. He has not yet set fire to Rome. He has not killed his mother, his wife, his tutors. Apart from that, it seems to me that enough cruelties escaped him to stop anyone misunderstanding him.

Some people have taken up the cause of Narcissus, and complained that I made him a very bad man and the confidant of Nero. One passage is a sufficient reply to them. 'Nero', says Tacitus, 'bore Narcissus' death impatiently, because this freedman fitted in marvellously well with the vices of the prince, which were still hidden.'

Others were scandalized that I had chosen a man as young as Britannicus as the hero of a tragedy. I have set out for them, in the preface to *Andromache*, Aristotle's views on the tragic hero; and suggested that far from being perfect, he ought always to exhibit some imperfection. But I will add here, for their benefit, that a young prince of seventeen, who has strong feelings, is much in love, who is very frank and very credulous, all ordinary qualities in a young man, seemed to me very capable of exciting pity. That is all I have in mind.

But, they say, this prince was only at the beginning of his fifteenth year when he died. He and Narcissus are being given two more years than they in fact lived. I should not have spoken of this objection, if it had not been made, rather warmly, by a man who has taken the liberty of making an emperor who reigned only eight years, reign instead for twenty years, although that is a much more considerable change in a chronology in which time is calculated by the time emperors have been on the throne.

Junia has critics too. They say that out of an old coquette by the name of Junia Silana, I have made a very well-behaved young girl. What reply would they make if I told them that this Junia is an invented character, like Emilia in *Cinna*, like Sabina in *Horace*? But what I have to say to them is that, if they had read their history properly, they would have found a Junia Calvina, one of Augustus' family, sister of Silanus, to whom Claudius had promised Octavia. This Junia was young, beautiful and, as Seneca says, 'the most agreeable of girls'. She loved her brother tenderly; 'and their enemies', Tacitus says, 'accused them both of incest, although they were guilty of nothing but a little indiscretion'. If I show her as more discreet than she was, I have yet to hear that it is forbidden to improve a character's morals, especially when it is someone relatively unknown.

It is thought strange that she should appear on the stage after the death of Britannicus. Certainly it shows great delicacy not to allow her four rather moving lines to say that she is going to see Octavia. But, they say, it wasn't worth bringing her back for that. Someone else could have reported the fact for her. They do not know that one of the rules of the theatre is to put into a narrative only things which cannot be acted out on the stage; and that all the classical dramatists bring on to the stage actors who have nothing to say, except that they are coming from one place or going back to another.

All that is no use, my critics say. The play finishes with the recital of the death of Britannicus, and one shouldn't listen to the rest. People listen to it all the same, and with as much attention as any ending of a tragedy. I have always understood that tragedy being the imitation of a complete action, in which several persons come together, this action is finished only when it is known in what situation these persons are left. That is the practice of Sophocles almost everywhere. So in the *Antigone* he takes as many lines to represent the fury of Haemon and the punishment of Creon after the death of that princess, as I took for the imprecations of Agrippina, the withdrawal of Junia, the punishment of Narcissus, and the despair of Nero, after the death of Britannicus.

What would one have to do to satisfy such exacting judges? The thing would be easy, though one might not like going against common sense. All that would be needed would be to depart from naturalness and plunge into the extraordinary. Instead of a simple plot, loaded with little matter, as ought to be the case with an action which takes place in a single day and which, as it advances by stages to its conclusion, is supported only by the interests, sentiments, and passions of the characters, one would have to stuff this same plot with a quantity of incidents which could not take less than a month, with a great number of theatrical devices, the more surprising the less probable they were, with an infinite number of declamations in which one would make the actors say the exact opposite of what they ought to say. One could, for example, show some drunken hero, who blithely wanted to make his mistress hate him, a Spartan who was a great talker, a conqueror who uttered nothing but amorous platitudes, a woman who gave conquerors lessons in haughtiness. That would no doubt be something to amuse all these gentlemen. But what would be said by the small number of sensible people I am trying to please? How should I dare to show my face, so to speak, before all these great men of classical times whom I have chosen as my models? For, to adopt a reflection from one ancient writer, that is the real audience we should be trying to please; and we should always be asking ourselves: 'What would Homer and Virgil say, if they read these lines? What would Sophocles say, if he saw this scene on the stage?' However that may be, I have not claimed the right to stop people talking against my works. It would have been no use making such a claim. 'It is for others to see how they want to talk about you,' Cicero says, 'but they will certainly talk.'

I only ask the reader to forgive me this little preface, which I have written to justify my tragedy to him. There is nothing more natural than defending oneself when one thinks one has been unjustly attacked. I observe that even Terence seems to have written prologues merely to justify himself against the criticisms of an ill-intentioned old poet, who used to organize opinion against him right up to the time when his comedies were presented. 'The play is beginning. There is shouting, etc.'

There is one difficulty which could have been raised which, however, no one has made to me. But what the audience missed could be noticed by readers. This is that I make Junia take a place among the Vestals, where, according to Aulus Gellius, no one was received below the age of six or above the age of ten. But the populace takes Junia under its protection, and I thought that, in view of her birth, her virtue, and her misfortunes, it could waive the age limit prescribed by the laws, as it waived the age-limit for the consulship, in the case of so many great men who had earned this privilege.

Finally, I am convinced that many other criticisms could have been levelled against me, criticisms I could only have made up my mind to profit by in the future. But I am very sorry for a man who works for public consumption. Those who see our faults most clearly are those who are most willing to conceal them. They forgive us the passages which have displeased them, for the sake of those which have given them pleasure. There is, on the contrary, nothing more unjust than someone who is ignorant. He always thinks that to admire is the lot of those who know nothing. He condemns a whole play for one scene of which he does not approve. He attacks even the most striking passages, to make people think he is clever; and however little resistance we put up to his opinions, he treats us as arrogant people who do not want to believe anybody, and he does not reflect that he prides himself more on a very bad piece of criticism, than we do on a rather good play. 'There is nothing more unjust than someone who is ignorant.'

SECOND PREFACE*
(1676)

OF all my tragedies this is the one at which I worked hardest. Yet I confess that its success did not at first answer to my hopes. It had hardly appeared on the stage before there arose a volume of criticisms which looked like destroying it. I thought myself that it would do less well in the future than my other tragedies. But what happened to this play in the end was what will always happen to works which have a certain merit. The criticisms disappeared; the play has remained. It is now the play of mine which the court and the public are most pleased to see again; and if I have done anything solid and deserving of some praise, most people who know about these things would agree that it is this same *Britannicus*.

I had in fact followed models which were an excellent basis for the picture I wished to give of the court of Agrippina and Nero. I had copied my characters from the greatest painter of antiquity, I mean Tacitus. I was then so full of my reading of that excellent historian, that there is hardly a striking feature in my tragedy the idea of which did not come from him. I had wished to put in this collection extracts from the best passages I have tried to imitate; but I found that these extracts would take up almost as much space as the tragedy itself. So the reader will have to be content with being referred to the author, whose works anyhow are in everybody's hands; and I shall merely indicate a few of the passages on each of the characters I introduce on the stage.

To begin with Nero, it must be remembered that he is here in the first years of his reign, which were happy ones, as is generally known. So it was not open to me to represent him as being as bad as he became later. Nor do I represent him as a virtuous man, because he never was one. He has not yet killed his mother, his wife, his tutors; but he has in him the seeds of all these crimes. He is beginning to want to loosen the yoke. He hates all of them, and he conceals his hatred from them by soft talk: 'formed by nature to veil his hatred under false blandishments'. In a word, he is here a budding monster, who does not yet dare to declare himself, and who tries to disguise his evil actions: 'Up to that

time, Nero sought to draw a veil over his vices and crimes.' He
could not bear Octavia, a princess of exemplary goodness and
virtue: 'whether it was fate, or the attraction of forbidden
pleasures; and the fear was that he would be so carried away
by his passions as to dishonour women of the most illustrious
birth'.

I make Narcissus his confidant. In that I have followed Tacitus,
who says that Nero 'bore Narcissus' death impatiently, because
this freedman fitted in marvellously well with the vices of the
prince, which were still hidden'. This passage proves two things:
it proves both that Nero was already vicious, but disguised his
vices, and that Narcissus supported him in his evil inclinations.

I chose Burrhus in order to contrast an honest man with this
court pest; and I chose him in preference to Seneca. For this
reason: they were both tutors of Nero in his youth, one for arms
and the other for letters; they were famous, Burrhus for his
experience in war and for the severity of his morals; Seneca for
his eloquence and his agreeable turn of mind. After his death
Burrhus was much regretted on account of his virtue; 'His death
left durable and great regret in Rome, which remembered his
virtues.'

Their whole effort was directed towards resisting the pride and
ferocity of Agrippina, 'who, blazing with all the passions of an
evil tyranny, had Pallas on her side'. That is all I am saying about
Agrippina, because there would be too much to say. She is the
character I have tried above all to give proper expression to, and
my tragedy is no less the disgrace of Agrippina than the death
of Britannicus. This death was a thunderbolt for her, and it
appeared, says Tacitus, by her fright and consternation, that she
was as innocent of this death as Octavia was. In him Agrippina
lost her last hope, and this crime made her fear a greater one: 'She
understood that her last resource had been taken from her, and
that this was a model for parricide.'

The age of Britannicus was so well known that there was no
question of my showing him otherwise than as a young man
who has strong feelings, is much in love, and who is very frank,
all ordinary qualities in a young man. 'He was fifteen, and it is
said that he was very intelligent, whether that was in fact true,
or whether his misfortunes made people think him so, without
his having been able to show signs of it.'

There is no reason to be surprised that he had close to him so bad a man as Narcissus; because orders had long ago been given that Britannicus should be attended only by people without loyalty or honour.

I have now only to speak of Junia. She is not to be confused with an old coquette called Junia Silana. Here it is another Junia, whom Tacitus calls Junia Calvina, one of Augustus' family, sister of Silanus, to whom Claudius had promised Octavia. This Junia was young, beautiful, and, as Seneca says, 'the most agreeable of girls'. She and her brother loved one another tenderly; 'and their enemies', Tacitus says, 'accused them both of incest, although they were guilty of nothing but a little indiscretion'. She lived on until the reign of Vespasian.

I make her take a place among the Vestals, although, according to Aulus Gellius, no one was ever received there under the age of six or above the age of ten. But the populace here takes Junia under its protection. And I thought that, in view of her birth, her virtue, and her misfortunes, it could waive the age limit prescribed by the laws, as it waived the age limit for the consulship in the case of so many great men who had earned that privilege.

THE CHARACTERS

NERO, the Emperor, son of Agrippina

BRITANNICUS, son of the Emperor Claudius

AGRIPPINA, widow of Domitius Aenobarbus, father of Nero, and, from her second marriage, widow of the Emperor Claudius

JUNIA, in love with Britannicus

BURRHUS, tutor to Nero

NARCISSUS, tutor to Britannicus

ALBINA, confidante to Agrippina

Guards

The scene is in Rome, in a room in Nero's palace.

ACT I

SCENE 1

Agrippina, Albina

ALBINA

    What, madam, while Nero is still asleep
    You must come here to wait till he is roused?
    Wandering alone through the palace without escort,
    Caesar's mother must keep watch at his door?
    Will you not go back to your apartment?   5

AGRIPPINA

    Albina, I cannot go away for a moment.
    I must wait for him here. He troubles me;
    That is enough to occupy my mind.
    All I foretold is happening as I said.
    Nero has come out against Britannicus.   10
    He is impatient now of all restraint.
    He has had enough of making himself loved;
    From now on his desire is to be feared.
    Britannicus is in his way, Albina;
    I can see that my turn is coming too.   15

ALBINA

    Yours! Yet Nero owes you the air he breathes,
    You brought him to empire when he had no hope of it!
    It was you disinherited the son of Claudius
    And named Domitius Caesar in his place.
    For him, Agrippina is everything;   20
    He owes you his love.

AGRIPPINA

                He owes it, yes.
    Everything points that way if he is generous;
    But if he is ungrateful, everything,
    Albina, points in the other direction.

ALBINA

    Can he be ungrateful, madam? His whole conduct   25
    Shows clearly he knows where his duty lies.

What has he said or done all these three years
Which does not promise Rome a perfect emperor?
Rome, after two years of his government,
Thinks she is back in the time of the consuls.   30
He rules like a father; the young Nero
Has all the virtues of the ageing Augustus.

AGRIPPINA
No, I have my interests but I am not unjust.
True, he has begun as Augustus ended;
But beware, the future may destroy the past   35
And he end in the way Augustus began.
It is no use him pretending: I read his looks,
Morose, savage, he is a true Domitian;
He combines the arrogance he has from them
With the pride of the Neros which is my part in him.   40
Tyranny always bears good fruit at first:
Caius delighted Rome for a time;
But his pretended kindness turned to fury
And Rome's delight was changed into horror.
What do I care if Nero, more consistent,   45
Should one day be a byword for his virtue?
Did I put him where he could guide the state
Only to steer as *plebs* and senate please?
The father of his country? Let him be so,
But not forget Agrippina is his mother.   50
Meanwhile, what can we call that lawless act
This very day has laid bare before us?
He knows, for love cannot remain a secret,
That Junia is adored by Britannicus,
And the same Nero who has so much virtue   55
Has Junia carried off at dead of night.
What does he want? Does hate or love inspire him?
Did he do that just for the pleasure of hurting them?
Or is it not rather that his malignity
Punishes them for the support I gave them?   60

ALBINA
Your support, madam?

AGRIPPINA
                    Stop, dear Albina.

I know that it was I who ruined them;
Britannicus, by right, should have had the throne;
He saw himself cast off by my intrigue.
And Junia had a brother, Silanus,   65
Whom Claudius intended for Octavia:
He killed himself because I stopped the marriage,
Descended from Augustus though he was.
Nero enjoys the booty, my reward
Is to hold the balance between him and them   70
So that one day, on the same principle,
Britannicus holds it between my son and me.

ALBINA
What you intend . . .

AGRIPPINA
                    Any port in a storm!
If this cannot stop Nero nothing will.

ALBINA
But such precautions, and against a son!   75

AGRIPPINA
If he did not fear me I should fear him.

ALBINA
Perhaps there is no cause to be frightened.
But, if Nero is not the son he should be,
That is a change which has escaped the rest of us
And these are secrets between Caesar and you.   80
Whatever new titles Rome bestows on him,
Nero accepts them only to share with you;
His generosity keeps nothing back.
His name is sacred, yours is sacred too.
The dull Octavia is rarely spoken of;   85
Livia had less honour from Augustus
Than you have from your son. Who, before Nero
Permitted the distinction to his mother,
Saw axes borne before her crowned with laurel?
What more do you want from his gratitude?   90

AGRIPPINA
A little less respect, more openness.
Albina, I resent all these shows.

I see my honours rise, my credit fall.
No, no, the time has gone when the young Nero
—Whom the court adored—conveyed its wishes to me;   95
When the whole burden of State fell upon me,
When it was my order assembled the senate
And, hidden from view, invisible but present,
In its deliberations I was all-powerful.
Uncertain still how Rome would take his actions,   100
Nero was then not drunk with greatness.
One day, one sad day, sticks in my memory,
When Nero was suddenly dazzled by his glory;
The ambassadors of many, many kings
Came to acknowledge him on behalf of the universe.   105
I was going to take my place on his throne beside him.
Whose advice he had had I do not know,
But some that were intent on my disgrace:
However that may be, when Nero saw me,
The resentment that he felt showed in his face.   110
I took it for an evil augury.
The ungrateful boy, respectfully insolent,
Rose to meet me and, running to embrace me,
Edged me away from the throne where I meant to sit.
Since that fatal moment, Agrippina's power   115
Has day by day declined by rapid steps.
Only the shadow remains, now all the cry
Is for Seneca and what Burrhus thinks best.

ALBINA

Ah, if your mind is so full of suspicion,
Why nourish a poison that will kill you?   120
At least ask Caesar for an explanation.

AGRIPPINA

Caesar will not now see me on his own.
In public, at fixed times, he gives me audience.
His answer is prescribed, his silence likewise.
I see two overseers, his masters and mine;   125
One or the other presides at all our interviews.
But avoid me as he will, I will pursue him.
I must make the most of his disarray.
Listen, Albina, the lock is turning; come,

Let's ask him why this girl was carried off   130
And, if we can, discover what he plans.
But oh, is that Burrhus coming out?

SCENE 2

Agrippina, Burrhus, Albina

BURRHUS
                                    Madam,
By the emperor's command, I was coming
To give you information about an order
Which might at first have struck you as alarming,   135
But is the consequence of prudent counsels
Of which Caesar wishes you to be aware.

AGRIPPINA
That being so, let's go in, and he will tell me.

BURRHUS
For the moment Caesar has withdrawn.
By another door, less public than this one,   140
The consuls have preceded you, both of them,
Madam. But allow me to go back to ask . . .

AGRIPPINA
No, I will not disturb his august secrets.
But perhapss you and I could have a word,
A somewhat franker one than we usually do?   145

BURRHUS
Burrhus is not the man to tell lies . . .

AGRIPPINA
How long would you keep the emperor from me?
Am I to see him now merely as a suitor?
Did I then raise your fortune so high
To set a barrier between my son and myself?   150
Dare you not trust him for a single moment?
Are you and Seneca in competition
To see who first can erase me from his memory?
When I put you in charge of him, was it for this,
That you should control the State in his name?   155
The more I think about it, the harder it is

To believe that you dare count me as your creature,
You whose ambition I could have left to wither
Amidst the obscure honours of some legion;
I, who succeed my ancestors on the throne, 160
The daughter, wife, sister, and mother of your masters.
What are you aiming at? Do you think that I
Made one emperor to subject myself to three?
Nero is not a child now. It is time he governed.
How much longer would you have the emperor fear you? 165
Must he see nothing except through your eyes?
Can he not follow his ancestors instead?
Let him choose either Augustus or Tiberius;
If he can, let him imitate Germanicus,
My father. I may not be one of those heroes 170
But there are virtues where I may show the way.
I can at least teach him to keep his distance
When he indulges in confidences with his subjects.

BURRHUS

I had intended, upon this occasion,
Only to excuse a single action of Caesar's; 175
But since without asking me to justify him
You make me answerable for the rest of his life,
I will answer you, madam, with all the frankness
Of an old soldier accustomed to speak plainly.
Yes, you put the young Caesar in my hands, 180
I agree, and certainly I should never forget it.
But did I swear to you to betray him?
Make him an emperor who could only obey?
No. It is not to you I must answer now.
He is no longer your son but the master of the world. 185
I am responsible to the Roman Empire
Which sees success or failure in my hands.
Ah, if it were ignorance he had to be taught,
Was there no one better than Seneca and I?
Why did you keep the flatterers away? 190
Why look among exiles for men to corrupt him?
The court of Claudius was not short of slaves,
If you wanted two, you could have found a thousand
All of them competing to drag him down.
They would have kept him a child long enough! 195

What have you to complain of, madam? You are revered;
People who swear by Caesar swear by his mother.
True, the emperor does not come every day
As one more courtier, to lay the world at your feet.
But should he, madam? Can his gratitude   200
Show in no other way than in dependence?
Is Nero, humble and timid still, to have
Nothing of Caesar Augustus but the name?
Shall I say it? Rome thinks him in the right.
Rome, so long at the mercy of three freedmen   205
And hardly alive under the yoke she bore,
Dates her liberty from the reign of Nero.
What am I saying? Virtue seems born again,
The empire is no longer one man's prey.
The people elect magistrates on the Field of Mars;   210
Caesar appoints leaders the soldiers want.
In the senate Thraseas, Corbulo in the army,
Are still innocent in spite of all their fame.
The wastes where once the senators were exiled
Are now inhabited by the old informers.   215
What does it matter whether Caesar still believes us
So long as our advice adds to his glory,
So long as, in the course of a flourishing reign,
Rome remains free and Caesar is all-powerful?
     But, madam, Nero can manage for himself,   220
I obey, not aspiring to instruct him.
His ancestors indeed are guides enough;
To do well, Nero has only to be himself,
Happy if his virtues, hand in hand,
Every year bring his first years back again.   225

AGRIPPINA

So, not daring to be certain of the future,
You think that Nero would be lost without you.
But you who, hitherto content with your handiwork,
Have just been bearing witness to his virtues,
Explain why, turning to violence when it suits him,   230
Nero has had Silanus' sister abducted.
Does he want only to mark with this ignominy
My ancestor's blood, which shows so well in Junia?
What is she accused of, what harm has she done,

To become a state criminal overnight?   235
She who, hitherto brought up without pride,
Would not have seen Nero if he had not seized her,
And would even have thought he was doing her a kindness
If she had had the happiness never to see him?

BURRHUS

I know she is not suspected of any crime.   240
But Caesar has still not condemned her of any,
Madam; and there is nothing here to offend her.
She is in a palace full of her ancestors.
You know that the rights her name carries with it
Could make her husband a rebellious prince: 245
That Caesar's blood should be allied to none
Except to those to whom Caesar wishes to entrust it;
And you will admit that it would not be right
That Augustus's niece should be married without his consent.

AGRIPPINA

I understand you. Nero is telling me,   250
Through you, that it is in vain for Britannicus
To count upon a choice that I have made.
In vain to stop him thinking of misfortune,
I have encouraged him to hope for the marriage:
To my confusion, Nero now seeks to show   255
That Agrippina promises what she cannot deliver.
Rome is too prejudiced in my favour;
He wishes by this insult to undeceive her,
So that the whole universe may learn in terror
Not to confuse my son with the emperor.   260
Let him, then. Yet I still dare say to him
That he should first make sure of his empire
And that, by reducing me to the necessity
Of trying my weak authority against his,
He is exposing his own, and that in the scales   265
My name perhaps may weigh more than he thinks.

BURRHUS

What, madam, you can still doubt his respect?
You are suspicious the moment he takes one step?
Does the emperor think that you are on Junia's side?
Does he think you in league with Britannicus?   270

What, you even come to support your enemies,
To find a pretext for quarrelling with him?
If one repeats a few words of his to you,
You do not hesitate to divide the empire?
Must you always fear him, and hardly embrace   275
Without falling into recriminations?
Ah, give up this censorious role of yours.
Treat him indulgently, as a mother may.
Do not draw attention to every small rebuff;
It will only warn the court to keep away from you.   280

AGRIPPINA

And who would value Agrippina's support
When Nero himself publishes my ruin,
When he appears to banish me from his presence,
When Burrhus dares to stop me at his door?

BURRHUS

Madam, I see that I am giving offence   285
And it is therefore time that I was silent.
There is injustice in grief, and all the reasons
Which do not soothe it make suspicions worse.
Here is Britannicus, I will make way,
Leave you to listen and pity his disgrace,   290
It may be, madam, to blame some of us
The emperor has consulted least of all.

SCENE 3

Agrippina, Britannicus, Narcissus, Albina

AGRIPPINA

Ah, prince! Where are you going? Why are you desperate
To throw yourself blindly among your enemies?
What are you looking for?

BRITANNICUS

               What am I looking for?   295
Gods! All I have lost, madam, is here.
Junia, surrounded by a thousand soldiers,
Has found herself dragged here amidst their threats.
What a sight for a timid girl like her!

What horror must she have felt, here in the palace!   300
She is being taken from me. What severity,
To separate hearts united in misfortune:
No doubt the intention is we should be deprived
Of the consolation of comforting one another.

AGRIPPINA

Enough. I feel your wrongs as my own.   305
You murmur: I have already made a complaint;
But I do not intend that helpless anger
Shall be the end of it: there is more to pay.
I cannot explain now. If you want to hear more,
Follow me to Pallas's house, where I will await you.   310

SCENE 4

Britannicus, Narcissus

BRITANNICUS

Shall I believe what she says, Narcissus,
And on her bare word take her as an arbitrator
Between her son and me? What do you think?
For is this not the same Agrippina
My father married and so ruined me?   315
And who, you tell me, hurried him from the world
Because he went too slowly for her plans?

NARCISSUS

No matter. Like you she feels herself outraged:
She undertook to give you Junia.
Your troubles are one, and so your interests must be.   320
Your regrets echo through the palace in vain.
As long as you are seen as a mere suppliant,
Uttering complaints but not inspiring fear;
While your resentments spend themselves in talk,
No doubt of it, you will complain for ever.   325

BRITANNICUS

Narcissus, ah, you know how little my mind
Intends to make a habit of servitude.
You know how little, since my violent fall,
I have renounced the empire, mine by right.

But I am still alone; my father's friends   330
Are as if strangers, my misfortune chills them,
My youth itself serves to keep at a distance
All those who in their hearts are still loyal.
This last year, when a little experience
Has made me understand my wretched lot,   335
What do I see around me but corrupt friends
Who watch my every step assiduously;
Who, chosen by Nero for this infamous trade,
Are trafficking my inmost secrets with him?
Narcissus, I am sold every day: 340
He knows my plans, he hears the words I speak;
He knows my heart as well as you yourself do.
How does it look to you, Narcissus?

NARCISSUS

                 Ah!
Who would be base enough? But, my lord,
It is for you to choose discreet friends   345
And not to tell the whole world your secrets.

BRITANNICUS

That's true, Narcissus, and yet such distrust
Is always hard for a great heart to learn;
The deception goes on. But I believe you,
Or rather, swear to believe no one but you.   350
My father, I remember, said you were zealous;
You alone, of his freedmen, are always loyal;
Your eyes, attentive to my every action,
Have saved me already from a thousand perils.
So go and see whether this latest storm   355
Has brought to life the courage of our friends.
Look in their eyes, observe their conversation;
See if I can expect their loyal assistance.
Observe with care, above all, with what precautions
Nero has had the princess Junia guarded.   360
Find out whether her lovely eyes are safe,
And whether I am still allowed to see her.
I meanwhile will seek out Nero's mother,
Who is with Pallas, like you my father's freedman.
I will see her, incite her, follow her,   365
Commit her further than she will want to go.

ACT II

SCENE 1

Nero, Burrhus, Narcissus, guards

NERO

To be plain, Burrhus: though she is wrong,
She is my mother, I will ignore her whims;
But have no intention of tolerating
The insolent minister who encourages them.   370
Pallas poisons my mother with his advice
And daily misleads Britannicus, my brother:
They listen to him secretly; if they were followed
They would perhaps be found with Pallas now.
It is too much. I must get him away from both.   375
For the last time, let him begone, leave now!
That is an order; by the end of the day
He is to be out of Rome and out of my court.
The security of the empire is at stake.
Go. You, Narcissus, come here. The rest can leave.   380

SCENE 2

Nero, Narcissus

NARCISSUS

The gods be thanked, my lord, you have Junia
And that will make you sure of the rest of the Romans.
Your enemies, their empty hopes defeated,
Have gone to Pallas's house to shed tears.
But what do I see? You look troubled, surprised,   385
More put out than even Britannicus.
What does it bode, this obscure melancholy,
These gloomy looks wandering here and there?
Fortune smiles on you and obeys your wishes.

NERO

The worst has happened, Narcissus. Nero's in love.   390

NARCISSUS
  You?

NERO
      This very moment, but for all my life.
  I love, I must say it, I worship Junia.

NARCISSUS
  You love her?

NERO
          Between desire and curiosity
  Last night I watched her arrival here,
  Sad, raising to heaven eyes wet with tears   395
  Which shone amidst the torches and the arms;
  Beautiful though she was in the simple attire
  Of a beauty who had just been snatched from sleep.
  What do you expect? Perhaps her negligée,
  The shadows, torches, shouts, and the silence   400
  And the wild looks of those violent men
  Set off the timid softness of her eyes:
  However that may be, the sight so took me
  I tried to speak to her, and my voice was gone.
  Motionless, filled with astonishment,   405
  I let her go past me to her apartment.
  I went back to mine. There, by myself,
  I tried hard not to think of her appearance.
  My eyes still saw her, I seemed to speak to her.
  I loved even the tears I made her weep.   410
  Sometimes, but too late, I asked her pardon;
  I had recourse to sighs, or even threats.
  That is how, thinking of nothing but my new love,
  My eyes waited for day without once closing.
  But perhaps my imagination flattered her;   415
  Perhaps she is not really so beautiful.
  Narcissus, what do you think?

NARCISSUS
                What, my lord,
  Can she have kept out of Nero's sight so long?

NERO
  You know she has, Narcissus. And either because
  She was angry and blamed me for her brother's death,   420

Or because her heart, in its austere pride,
Wanted to keep her dawning beauty from us,
True to her grief, and shut away in shadows,
She hid from us even her reputation;
It is this virtue, a novelty in this court,   425
Which irritates me, she is so steady in it.
Narcissus, there's not a single woman in Rome
Not honoured, or made vainer, by my love,
None, the first moment she dares trust her looks,
Does not attempt to try them out on Caesar.   430
And yet, alone in her palace, the modest Junia
Regards their honours as an ignominy,
Holds back, perhaps not deigning to find out
Whether Caesar can be loved, or knows how to love?
Tell me, does Britannicus love her?

NARCISSUS

                                        You ask,   435
My lord?

NERO

                    He is so young, does he know himself?
Does he know the poison of an enchanting glance?

NARCISSUS

My lord, love does not always wait for reason.
Have no doubt, he loves her. Already her charms
Have taught his eyes the use of tears. He knows   440
How to meet all her slightest wishes half-way;
Perhaps, already, how to persuade her.

NERO

What are you saying? Has he some hold on her?

NARCISSUS

I do not know, my lord, but I can tell you
I have sometimes seen him storm out of here,   445
His heart full of anger he concealed from you,
Bewailing the ingratitude of a court
Where he is shunned, and shedding bitter tears,
Tired of your greatness and his servitude.
Undecided between impatience and fear.   450
He was off to see Junia and he came back happy.

NERO

The worse for him, the more he pleases her,
Narcissus! He had better wish her angry:
Nero will not take jealousy lying down!

NARCISSUS

You? Why should you be anxious, my lord?   455
Junia perhaps pitied and shared his troubles:
His are the only tears she has ever seen;
But my lord, now that you open her eyes,
She sees at close quarters all your splendour;
Around you she sees kings without diadems,   460
Anonymous in the crowd, and her lover himself,
All proud to have even a look from you
Although it only falls on them by chance;
When she sees you, in this degree of glory,
Come sighing to her that she has won you,   465
Master, you have only, with a heart so charmed,
To order her to love you, and she will.

NERO

How many difficulties I have to expect,
With everyone against me!

NARCISSUS

                                 What prevents you,
My lord?   470

NERO

Everything: Octavia, Agrippina,
Burrhus, Seneca, and the whole of Rome,
And besides that, my three years of virtue.
Not that I feel anything for Octavia
Which could hold me to her or make me pity her youth: 475
My eyes have seen enough of her attentions
And do not often deign to watch her tears.
I should be too happy if a divorce
Were to rid me of a yoke that was imposed on me!
Heaven itself seems secretly to condemn her: 480
Though for four years she has prayed, the gods
Give no sign that her virtue touches them;
They do not honour her with a child, Narcissus;
The empire wants an heir and does not get one.

NARCISSUS

    Why not repudiate her straight away?   485
    The empire, your heart, and all condemn Octavia.
    Your ancestor Augustus wanted Livia:
    It took a double divorce to unite them:
    You owe the empire to that happy divorce.
    Tiberius, brought into the family by marriage,   490
    Dared to repudiate Augustus's daughter.
    You alone fly in the face of your desires
    And dare not secure your pleasure by a divorce!

NERO

    But Agrippina is implacable!
    Already my love makes me imagine her   495
    Bringing Octavia to me and, her eyes ablaze,
    Swearing a marriage made by her is sacred,
    Then, with a more brutal attack on my feelings,
    Telling me a long tale about my ingratitudes.
    How am I to manage that awkward interview?   500

NARCISSUS

    Are you not, my lord, your master and hers too?
    Are we always to see you doing as she bids you?
    Live and reign for yourself and not for her.
    Are you afraid ... My lord, you cannot fear her:
    You have just banished her proud adviser, Pallas,   505
    Pallas who is impudent because she supports him.

NERO

    Out of her sight, I give orders, I threaten,
    I listen to your advice and dare approve it,
    I work myself up and try to defy her;
    But (and I show myself to you as I am),   510
    As soon as I have the bad luck to see her,
    Either I still dare not resist her eyes
    Where I have so long looked to know my duty,
    Or I cannot forget the many benefits
    I have from her, and lay them at her feet: 515
    However it may be, try as I will
    My mind is powerless before her own;
    It is to free myself from this dependence
    That I avoid her everywhere, give offence

And sometimes even try to provoke her,   520
So that, as I avoid her, she will me.
But do not stop here too long, Narcissus;
Britannicus may suspect you of duplicity.

NARCISSUS
No, no, Britannicus trusts me entirely.
He thinks that I am seeing you by his order,   525
My lord, to find out how things stand for him;
He wants to know your secrets through my lips.
Above all, anxious to see his love again
He expects help from me in that matter.

NERO
And so he shall have. Take him the good news: 530
He will see her.

NARCISSUS
                My lord, banish him, far from her.

NERO
I have my reasons, Narcissus, you may be sure
He will pay dear for the pleasure of seeing her.
But boast to him how cleverly you arranged it
And how for his sake I have been misled,   535
And he is seeing her without my orders.
But now the door is opening; here she is.
Go find your master now and bring him here.

SCENE 3

Nero, Junia

NERO
You look troubled, madam, and change colour.
Do you see some ill omen in my eyes?   540

JUNIA
My lord, I must confess my mistake:
I was going to see Octavia, not the emperor.

NERO
I know, madam, and was a little envious
To hear how kind you were to Octavia.

JUNIA
  You, my lord?

NERO
                          Can you imagine, madam,   545
  That none but Octavia has eyes to see you?

JUNIA
  Of whom else, my lord, should I beg a favour?
  Or ask what my crime is, unknown to me?
  You who are punishing it must know, my lord:
  Tell me what outrages I have committed.   550

NERO
  What, madam, is it so small an offence
  To have hidden yourself from me for so long?
  These treasures with which heaven has embellished you,
  Were they given to you only for you to bury them?
  Happy Britannicus must be alarmed: 555
  His love, and your charms, grow where I cannot see them.
  Why have you shut me out until today,
  Banished in my own court from all that glory?
  It is said, too, you allow him, quite freely,
  Madam, to say all that is in his mind: 560
  For I cannot believe that, without consulting me,
  The severe Junia ventured to flatter him,
  Nor yet consented to love and to be loved
  Without my knowing otherwise than by hearsay.

JUNIA
  I will not deny, my lord, that he has sometimes   565
  Let his sighs speak what was in his heart.
  He has not turned his eyes away from a girl
  Who is all that remains of a famous family.
  He may remember that in happier times
  His father named me as a fit bride for him.   570
  He loves me, so obeying the emperor his father,
  And, I may say, you and your mother too:
  Your wishes are always in accord with hers ...

NERO
  My mother has her plans, madam, I mine.
  Enough of Claudius and Agrippina: 575
  It is not they who will make up my mind.

It is for me alone, madam, to answer you,
And I intend to choose a husband for you.

JUNIA

Ah, my lord, do you think any other alliance
Would shame the Caesars to whom I owe my birth?   580

NERO

No, madam; the husband I am talking of
Would bring disgrace to no one by the marriage
And you need not blush to accept his love.

JUNIA

Who, my lord, is this husband?

NERO

                           It is I.

JUNIA

You!

NERO

    I would, madam, choose another if   585
I knew a name which stood higher than Nero's.
Yes, to make a choice you could agree to,
I have surveyed the court, Rome, and the empire.
The more I looked, and the more I look
To see into whose hands I could convey this treasure,   590
The more I see that Caesar alone is worthy
And that only he must have this happiness;
He can entrust you to no other hands
Than those to which Rome committed the entire world.
You yourself look to your early years for guidance.   595
Claudius intended you for his son;
But that was in a day when the whole empire
Was to have passed in due course to his son as heir.
The gods have spoken. You must not oppose them
But go the same way as the empire has gone.   600
Useless for me to have been honoured with that gift
If your heart was to be separated from it,
If your charms were not there to soothe my cares,
If, while I spend in watches and alarms
Days others envy, but which should be pitied,   605
I cannot sometimes throw myself at your feet.

The thought of Octavia need not be a shadow:
All Rome speaks for you as I do myself,
Repudiates Octavia and would have me undo
A marriage which the heavens will not acknowledge.   610
Think therefore, madam, and weigh for yourself
This choice so worthy of a prince who loves you,
Worthy of your fair eyes so long imprisoned,
Worthy of the universe, which you cannot refuse.

JUNIA

My lord, I cannot but be astonished.   615
I see myself, in the course of a single day,
Brought to these precincts like a criminal,
Then, when I timidly appear before you,
Hardly daring to trust my own innocence,
You suddenly offer me Octavia's place.   620
Yet I dare claim not to have merited
Either the honour or the indignity.
And can you, my lord, hope that a girl
Whose first days saw her family extinguished,
Who, nursing her grief in obscurity,   625
Has trained herself to virtue to match her misfortune,
Could suddenly pass from so profound a night
Into a rank where the world's eyes are on her
—I who could not bear it even from a distance,
A rank whose majesty another graces.   630

NERO

I have already told you I repudiate her.
So be less timid or at least less modest.
Do not accuse me of choosing blindly:
I'll answer for you, you have only to consent.
Call to mind from what blood you are descended,   635
And do not prefer to the solid glory
Of honours Caesar has designed for you
The glory of a refusal you will be sorry for.

JUNIA

Heaven knows, my lord, the bottom of my heart,
I am not looking for a senseless glory.   640
I know how great the gifts are that you offer;
But the more splendour this rank shed on me,

The more it would disgrace me and expose
The crime of having robbed the rightful owner.

NERO

You are assiduous in her interests,　　　　　　　645
Madam, friendship indeed can go no further.
Let us have no deceptions, no pretences.
The sister matters less to you than the brother,
And as for Britannicus . . .

JUNIA

　　　　　　　　　　　He matters to me,
My lord, I have made no attempt to hide it.　　　650
Sincerity no doubt is indiscreet,
But my lips always speak for my heart.
Away from court, I have not had to think,
My lord, that I must be an expert in pretence.
I love Britannicus. I was meant for him　　　　655
When marrying him meant marrying the empire.
But the misfortune which set him aside,
His cancelled honours and deserted palace,
A court avoiding him because of his fall,
Are all so many bonds to hold Junia.　　　　　660
Everything you see is fashioned to your will;
Your serene days are all passed in pleasures;
The empire will supply you inexhaustibly;
Or, if some trouble interrupts the flow,
The whole universe, anxious they should continue,　665
Will rush to wipe it from your memory.
Britannicus is alone. When he has troubles,
No one except myself is interested;
His only pleasures, my lord, are a few tears
In which, sometimes, his troubles are forgotten.　670

NERO

Those are the pleasures and the tears I envy,
And anyone else would pay for them with his life.
But I am treating the prince in a gentler manner:
Madam, he will soon appear before you.

JUNIA

Ah my lord, I have always trusted your virtues.　675

NERO
> I could forbid him entry to this place;
> But, madam, I prefer to avert the danger
> Which his resentment could involve him in.
> I do not want to ruin him. Better he should
> Learn of his sentence from the lips he loves.   680
> If you value his life, break with him now,
> Without his having cause to think me jealous.
> Take the blame for his banishment on yourself;
> Either by what you say, or by your silence,
> Or at least by your coldness, make him think   685
> That he should take his love and hope elsewhere.

JUNIA
> I! It is I must pronounce this severe sentence!
> My lips have sworn the opposite a thousand times.
> Even if I could betray myself so far,
> My eyes, my lord, would not let him obey me.   690

NERO
> I shall be hidden here, I shall see you, madam.
> Lock your love in the bottom of your heart.
> Everything that passes between you I shall see:
> I shall understand looks you will think dumb:
> And he will infallibly be lost   695
> If any sigh or gesture from you pleases him.

JUNIA
> Ah, if I may express a wish, my lord,
> Allow me never to see him again.

SCENE 4

Nero, Junia, Narcissus

NARCISSUS
> Britannicus, my lord, seeks the princess;
> He is coming.

NERO

> > Let him come.

JUNIA

> > > My lord!

NERO

                                        I leave you.   700
  His fate depends on you more than on me.
  When you see him, madam, remember I see you.

SCENE 5

Junia, Narcissus

JUNIA
  Oh, dear Narcissus, run and meet your master.
  Tell him ... But I am lost, I see him here.

SCENE 6

Junia, Britannicus, Narcissus

BRITANNICUS
  Madam, what happy chance brings me to you?   705
  Can I enjoy your company for a moment?
  Yet, pleasure though it is, what grief consumes me!
  Can I, alas, hope ever to see you again?
  Must I steal, by a thousand twists and turns,
  What your eyes gave me freely every day?   710
  What a night! What a waking! All your tears,
  Your presence, have not subdued these insolent bullies!
  What was your lover doing? What envious demon
  Denied me the honour of dying before your eyes?
  Alas! Did you, when you were so frightened,   715
  Address any secret complaint to me?
  My princess, did you deign to wish me there?
  Did you think what grief you were going to cause me?
  You say nothing? What a reception! What coldness!
  Is that how your eyes console my disgrace?   720
  Speak: we're alone. Our enemy has been tricked:
  While I talk with you, he is otherwise occupied.
  Let us make the most of this welcome absence.

JUNIA
  You are in a place which is full of his power.
  These very walls, my lord, may have eyes;   725
  The emperor is never absent here.

BRITANNICUS
    And how long, madam, have you been so fearful?
    What! does your love admit itself a prisoner?
    Where is that heart which always swore to me
    It would make Nero himself envy our love?   730
    But, madam, put aside this useless fear:
    Good faith is not yet dead in every heart:
    Everyone seems to sympathize with my anger,
    And Nero's mother has declared for us.
    Rome itself is offended by his conduct . . .   735

JUNIA
    Ah, my lord, your words belie your thoughts.
    You have yourself told me a thousand times
    That Rome with one voice spoke in his praise.
    You always paid some tribute to his virtue.
    No doubt it is your grief makes you talk thus.   740

BRITANNICUS
    Your words astonish me, I must admit.
    I did not seek you out to hear him praised.
    What! I have only just stolen a moment
    To confide in you how grief overwhelms me,
    And this precious moment is consumed   745
    By praise of the enemy who oppresses me!
    One day, and you are so unlike yourself!
    Even your looks have learned to say nothing!
    What do I see? You dare not meet my eyes?
    Can you like Nero? Can I now be odious?   750
    Ah, if I thought . . . Madam, by all the gods!
    Explain this trouble you inflict on me.
    Speak. Have you entirely forgotten me?

JUNIA
    Withdraw, my lord, the emperor is coming.

BRITANNICUS
    After such a blow, Narcissus, whom may I trust?   755

SCENE 7

Nero, Junia, Narcissus

NERO
  Madam ...

JUNIA
     No, my lord, I can hear nothing.
  You are obeyed: at least let me weep;
  The tears will not be seen by his eyes.

SCENE 8

Nero, Narcissus

NERO
  Well! you can see how violent their love is,
  Narcissus; it showed even in her silence.   760
  She loves my rival, that I must admit,
  But I shall enjoy making him give up hope.
  I have a charming picture of his suffering;
  And I have seen him doubt his lady's heart.
  I'll follow her. My rival only waits for you   765
  To burst out afresh. Run after him,
  Go, and torment him with new suspicions;
  While I watch Junia's tears of adoration,
  Make him pay dear for a happiness
  He does not know is his.

NARCISSUS, *alone.*
          A second time   770
  Fortune summons Narcissus; will he hear?
  I will follow to the end her offered favours
  And ruin beggars to be rich myself.

ACT III

SCENE 1

Nero, Burrhus

BURRHUS
Pallas, my lord, will obey.

NERO
And my mother,
How did she view this humbling of his pride? 775

BURRHUS
You may be sure, my lord, she feels this blow
And will shortly show it by her reproaches.
Her fury has long threatened to explode:
May it go no further than useless cries!

NERO
What, then you think she may be plotting something? 780

BURRHUS
Agrippina, my lord, must always be feared:
Rome and the army worship her ancestors;
They see Germanicus her father still;
She knows her power, and you know her courage;
What makes me fear her more, my lord, is this: 785
That you yourself give her occasion for anger
And furnish her with arms to use against you.

NERO
I, Burrhus?

BURRHUS
My lord, this love which possesses you . . .

NERO
I understand you, Burrhus. There is no cure.
My heart has told me more than you can tell me. 790
My love is a necessity.

BURRHUS
You imagine it so,
My lord and, content with slight resistance,
You fear an ill which is small in its beginnings.

But if your heart, firmly attached to duty,
Refused all parley with its enemy;   795
If you considered the glory of your early years,
And deigned, my lord, a little to remember
Octavia's virtues, which deserve better than this,
And her chaste love, still strong though you despise her;
If, above all, you avoided Junia,   800
Condemning your eyes to some days of absence:
Believe me, however love seems to charm you,
One does not love, my lord, unless one wants to.

NERO

I will believe you, Burrhus, when there is danger
And what is at stake is the glory of our arms,   805
Or when, in calmer times, in the senate,
The safety of the State calls for decisions:
For that, I shall rely on your experience.
But, believe me, love is another matter,
Burrhus; and I should not find it easy   810
To bring your severe mind to bear so low.
Goodbye. It's too painful, away from Junia.

SCENE 2

BURRHUS, *alone.*

So now, Burrhus, Nero shows his true colours.
This wild beast that you hoped to hold in check
Is now prepared to break through your restraints.   815
And what excesses now may be unleashed!
O gods! Who can I turn to in this trouble?
Seneca, who should be of assistance,
Is out of Rome, unaware of the danger.
But yet! If Agrippina has any tenderness,   820
I could . . . A happy chance has sent her to me.

SCENE 3

Agrippina, Burrhus, Albina

AGRIPPINA

So, Burrhus, I was wrong in my suspicions?

And you are famous for your lofty precepts!
Pallas is exiled, his crime was, perhaps,
Raising your master to be emperor.   825
You know it well enough: he ruled Claudius
And so it was that my son was adopted.
Now, it seems, Nero's wife is given a rival
And he is told his marriage counts for nothing:
A fine thing for a minister who hates flatterers,   830
Chosen to keep his youthful heat in check,
To flatter it himself, and to encourage him
To scorn his mother and forget his wife!

BURRHUS

Madam, so far the accusation is premature.
The emperor has done nothing inexcusable.   835
Blame Pallas for his exile: it was necessary:
His pride had long since called for this reward;
The emperor does no more than carry out,
Regretfully, what the court secretly wants.
The other matter is not beyond repair: 840
Octavia's tears can be dried up at the source.
But calm your indignation. You could rather
Bring back her husband by a gentler way:
Menaces, cries, will make him wilder still.

AGRIPPINA

It is no use trying to shut my mouth.   845
I see my silence arouses your contempt;
That is too much from a creature I have made.
Agrippina has other supports than Pallas;
Heaven has left me enough to avenge my fall.
Claudius' son begins to feel the effects   850
Of crimes for which I alone am responsible.
Rest assured, I will show him to the army,
Before the soldiers' eyes express my pity
For his wronged childhood, urging them to follow me
In expiating their faults as I do mine.   855
On one hand they will see an emperor's son
Appealing for the loyalty they swore to his family,
And they will hear the daughter of Germanicus;
On the other hand, the son of Enobarbus,

Supported by Seneca and by Burrhus the tribune,   860
Both of whom I called back from exile,
Sharing supreme authority before my eyes.
I shall make public all our common crimes
And tell how devious were the ways I led him.
To make his power and yours odious   865
I shall confirm the most injurious rumours:
I shall confess to exiles, assassinations,
Even poison, all . . .

BURRHUS
                    Madam, they won't believe you.
They will challenge your evidence as the stratagem
Of an offended witness who accuses herself.   870
As for me, the first to second your plans,
Who made the army swear, their hands in his,
I do not at all repent having done my duty.
Madam, it is a son succeeding his father.
By adopting Nero, Claudius freely chose   875
To give his son and your son equal rights.
Rome was entitled to choose him. Without injustice
She chose Tiberius, adopted by Augustus,
And young Agrippa, who was of his blood,
Found that he was excluded, he had no claim.   880
His power rests on so many firm foundations
That today even you cannot upset it.
If he takes my advice, madam, his kindness
Will soon make you unwilling to disturb it.
I have begun my task, I mean to go on.   885

SCENE 4

Agrippina, Albina

ALBINA
Your suffering carries you away, madam.
I only hope the emperor does not hear of it!

AGRIPPINA
I only hope he lets me set my eyes on him!

ALBINA
Madam, in the gods' names, conceal your anger.

What! For the sister's sake, or the brother's,   890
Must you sacrifice your own peace of mind?
Must you manage even Caesar's love affairs?

AGRIPPINA

What! you cannot see how they drag me down,
Albina? It is to me they are giving a rival.
Soon, if I do not break this fatal connection,   895
My place is taken, I shall no longer count.
Octavia's title has been an empty one,
She has been useless at court, and remained unknown.
Favours and honours were dispensed by me;
It was to me that mortals had to pray.   900
Another woman has captured Caesar's affection;
She will reign as a wife and as a mistress.
The fruit of so much care, the pomp of the Caesars,
All will reward a single look of hers.
What am I saying? I am avoided, abandoned . . .   905
Ah, I cannot, Albina, bear the thought of it.
Even should I hasten the fatal decree of heaven,
Nero, ungrateful Nero . . . But see, his rival!

SCENE 5

Britannicus, Agrippina, Narcissus, Albina

BRITANNICUS

Our common enemies are not invincible,
Madam, and there are hearts which feel our ills.   910
Your friends and mine, hitherto so discreet,
While we were wasting our time in vain regrets,
Stirred by the anger which injustice arouses,
Have just now been confiding in Narcissus.
Nero is not yet in peaceful possession   915
Of the wretch he loves at my sister's expense.
If you still feel the wrong to her as I do,
The perjurer can still be taught his duty.
Half of the senate has taken sides with us:
Sylla, Piso, Plautus.

AGRIPPINA

                    Prince, what is this?   920
Sylla, Piso, Plautus! the leading nobles!

BRITANNICUS

Madam, I see you do not like this talk
And that your anger, trembling and irresolute,
Already fears the success of its demands.
No, you have managed my disgrace too well: 925
Fear no bold stroke by any friend of mine.
I have none any more, you have been too careful
To turn them from me or have long seduced them.

AGRIPPINA

My lord, give less credit to your suspicions:
All depends now on our acting as one.   930
I have promised, that's enough. Despite your enemies,
You will not find I go back on my word.
Nero has gone too far to escape my anger:
Sooner or later he must listen to me.
I shall try force and gentleness in turn;   935
Or I myself, taking your sister with me,
Will spread abroad my fear and her alarms,
And win all hearts to take sides with her tears.
Goodbye. I will lay siege to Caesar from all sides.
My advice to you is, keep out of his sight.   940

SCENE 6

Britannicus, Narcissus

BRITANNICUS

Have you not flattered me with a false hope?
Can I have confidence in your story,
Narcissus?

NARCISSUS

                    Yes. But this is not the place,
My lord, to unfold this mystery to you.
Let's go. What are you waiting for?

BRITANNICUS

                                  What, Narcissus?   945
   Alas!

NARCISSUS
     Explain yourself.

BRITANNICUS
                           If you could somehow
   Arrange for me to see …

NARCISSUS
                  Whom?

BRITANNICUS
                          I blush, but
   I should await my destiny more calmly.

NARCISSUS
   After all I have said, you still think her faithful?

BRITANNICUS
   No, Narcissus, I think her ungrateful, criminal,   950
   I should be angry with her; but, in spite of myself,
   I do not blame her as I ought to do.
   My stubborn heart excuses her, invents
   Reasons for her wild conduct, worships her;
   I cannot believe it of her, yet I would,   955
   And, if I could, hate her with a calm hatred.
   Who will believe that a heart which seems so great
   And which from childhood hated a faithless court,
   Should throw aside its glory and, the first day,
   Work at a treachery unheard of even there?   960

NARCISSUS
   And who knows whether, in her long seclusion,
   She was not heartlessly planning her victory?
   She knew she could not always hide from the emperor
   And perhaps fled to be the more sought after,
   To incite Nero by the haughty mien   965
   Of a pride hitherto invincible.

BRITANNICUS
   So I cannot see her?

NARCISSUS

           My lord, at this moment
She is listening to the addresses of her new lover.

BRITANNICUS

Well, let us go, Narcissus. But here she is!

NARCISSUS

Ah, gods! I must tell the emperor the news.   970

SCENE 7

Britannicus, Junia

JUNIA

Withdraw at once, my lord, avoid the anger
Which my determination has excited.
Nero is furious with you. I have escaped
Only because your mother is detaining him.
Goodbye; without offence to my love,   975
Keep yourself for the pleasure of one day
Hearing me justify my course of action.
Your image is ceaselessly in my mind:
Nothing can banish it.

BRITANNICUS

           I understand you:
Madam, my flight will give you what you want,   980
To leave the field clear for your new fancies.
No doubt when you see me a secret shame
Allows you only an uncertain joy.
Well then, I'll go.

JUNIA

          My lord, without imputing . . .

BRITANNICUS

Ah, you should at least have argued longer!   985
I am not complaining that a common friendship
Should take the side that has the kiss of fortune,
Or that you should be dazzled by the empire
And want to enjoy it at my sister's expense;

But that, while you were impressed, like anyone else,   990
With these splendours, you long appeared to me
As one who saw the hollowness of it all:
No, I confess it still, my desperate heart
Was prepared for any misfortune but this one.
I saw injustice built upon my ruin   995
And heaven itself the accomplice of my persecutors.
So many horrors had not exhausted its anger,
Madam: I did not know you could forget me.

JUNIA

In happier times, I would—justly—lose patience
And make you sorry for your lack of trust.   1000
But Nero threatens you: in this instant danger,
My lord, I have better things to do than trouble you.
Go, but be reassured, do not complain:
Nero was listening and ordered me to pretend.

BRITANNICUS

What! the cruel . . .

JUNIA

                     Witnessed the whole interview;   1005
He was watching my face narrowly all the time,
Prepared to let his vengeance loose on you
At any sign that we two were in league.

BRITANNICUS

Nero was listening to us! Madam, but, oh!
Your eyes could have pretended and not deceived me.   1010
They could have told me who was responsible.
Is love dumb, has it only one way of speaking?
A look could have preserved me from that pain!
You had only . . .

JUNIA

               I had to keep quiet and save you.
How many times, alas, since I must tell you,   1015
My heart was on the point of telling you all!
How many sighs did I interrupt
By avoiding your eyes, which mine sought all the time!
What torture to keep quiet when you were there,
And I hearing you groan, yet having to hurt you,   1020

When with a look I could have consoled.
But what tears would that look have sent down my cheeks!
Thinking of that, I was restless and troubled
And felt I was not dissimulating enough.
I feared the pallor of my frightened face;   1025
It seemed to me my looks showed too much grief.
All the time I thought Nero was coming,
Angry, reproaching me for trying to please you.
I feared I could not keep my love concealed;
I wished indeed that I had never loved.   1030
Alas, he knows too much for his own happiness
—And for ours—about my heart and yours.
Once again, go, and keep out of his sight;
You shall hear more later of what I think.
There are a thousand secrets to explain.   1035

BRITANNICUS
It is too much already. I understand,
Madam, my happiness, my crime, your goodness!
And do you know all you are giving up for me?
When shall I expiate this reproach at your feet?

JUNIA
What are you doing? Alas, here is your rival.   1040

SCENE 8
Nero, Britannicus, Junia

NERO
Continue, prince, with your charming transports.
Madam, I can imagine your kindness
From the way he thanks you: I have seen him clasp your knees.
But he should give some thanks to me too:
This place suits him well, and I keep you here   1045
To make such conversations easier for him.

BRITANNICUS
I can lay my grief and joy at her feet.
Anywhere where her kindness consents to see me;
And the appearance of this place where you are keeping her
Should not be unfamiliar to me.   1050

NERO

    And what do you see here which does not warn you
    That I am to be respected and obeyed?

BRITANNICUS

    This place saw us both growing up, but not
    With me obeying, and you lording it over me;
    And did not expect, when it saw us born,   1055
    That one day Domitius would speak to me as a master.

NERO

    So it is fate crosses all our wishes:
    I obeyed then, you are obeying now.
    If you have not yet learned to submit,
    You are still young, you can be taught a lesson.   1060

BRITANNICUS

    And who will teach me?

NERO

                      The whole empire together,
    Rome.

BRITANNICUS

           And does Rome count as among your rights
    All the cruelties of injustice and violence,
    Imprisonments, carrying off by force, divorce?

NERO

    Rome does not let her curious eyes stray   1065
    As far as the secrets I conceal from her.
    Imitate her respect.

BRITANNICUS

               Her thoughts are known.

NERO

    But she keeps quiet. Imitate her silence.

BRITANNICUS

    So Nero is beginning to be himself.

NERO

    Nero begins to be tired of your speeches.   1070

BRITANNICUS

    Everyone should be glad of a happy reign.

NERO

    Never mind happiness, as long as they fear me.

BRITANNICUS

If I know Junia, sentiments of that kind
Will not win or deserve her praise or approval.

NERO

At least, if I do not know how to please her,   1075
I know how to punish a headstrong rival.

BRITANNICUS

What danger soever overwhelms me,
Her enmity alone can make me flinch.

NERO

Try wishing for it: that is my advice.

BRITANNICUS

All I want is the happiness of pleasing her.   1080

NERO

She has promised you that you will always please her.

BRITANNICUS

At least I know better than to spy on her:
I let her say whatever she will about me
And do not hide myself to shut her mouth.

NERO

I understand you. Guards!

JUNIA

                                        What are you doing?   1085
It is your brother. A jealous lover, alas!
My lord, think, he has a thousand misfortunes:
Can this one happiness excite your envy?
Only allow me, to bring you together,
To hide from your eyes and withdraw from his.   1090
My going will bring an end to your dissensions;
My lord, I will find a place among the Vestals.*
Dispute no more over my unfortunate wishes;
Let no one but the gods be troubled by them.

NERO

Madam, this is a strange and sudden notion.   1095
Guards, make sure she goes back to her apartments
And keep Britannicus in his sister's.

BRITANNICUS

That is how Nero tries to win a heart.

JUNIA
    Prince, no more, let us bow before the storm.

NERO
    Guards, obey me without further delay.   1100

SCENE 9

Nero, Burrhus

BURRHUS
    What do I see? O heavens!

NERO, *without seeing Burrhus.*
                              They will love all the more.
    I recognize the hand which brought them together:
    Agrippina presented herself before me
    And spent so long saying what she had to say
    Only in order to play this odious trick.   1105
    Find out whether my mother is still here.
    Burrhus, I want her kept in this palace;
    In place of her own guards, I give her mine.

BURRHUS
    My lord, without hearing her? A mother?

NERO
                                        Stop.
    I do not know, Burrhus, what you are plotting;   1110
    But, in the last few days, everything I want
    Finds in you a censor to contradict me.
    You shall answer for it or, if you do not,
    Others shall answer to me for her and Burrhus.

ACT IV

SCENE 1

Agrippina, Burrhus

BURRHUS

Yes, madam, you will have time for your defence.   1115
Caesar himself agrees to hear you out.
If his order confines you to the palace,
It is perhaps because he intends to talk with you.
Be that as it may, if I may say what I think,
Do not remember that he may have offended you: 1120
Be ready, rather, to open your arms to him;
Defend yourself, madam; do not accuse him.
You see, the court looks only in his direction.
Although he is your son, even your handiwork,
He is your emperor and you are, like us,   1125
Subject to the power he received from you.
Accordingly as he threatens or makes much of you,
The court either keeps away from you or flocks around;
It is his support they want when they ask for yours.
But here is the emperor.

AGRIPPINA

                                    Leave me with him.   1130

SCENE 2

Agrippina, Nero

AGRIPPINA, *taking a seat.*

Come closer, Nero, and sit here with me.
I am told I should answer your suspicions.
I do not know what crime has been fastened on me:
All that I have committed, I will explain.
      You are reigning. You know well how great a distance   1135
Your birth had set between you and the empire.
My ancestors' rights, consecrated by Rome,
Would have been empty titles without me.

When the condemned mother of Britannicus
Allowed Claudius's marriage to be disputed,   1140
Among so many beauties competing for him
Who begged his freedmen to support their claims,
I wanted his bed for one reason only,
To leave you on the throne where I should be.
I swallowed my pride and went to solicit Pallas.   1145
His master, whom I fondled every day,
Imperceptibly caught from his niece's eyes
The love I meant his tenderness to lead to.
But this tie of blood which connected us
Turned Claudius away from an incestuous bed: 1150
He did not dare to marry his brother's daughter.
The senate was seduced; a less stringent law
Put Claudius in my bed and Rome at my feet.
That achieved much for me, but nothing for you.
I made you follow my steps into his family: 1155
It was I who appointed you his son-in-law
And gave you his daughter, while Silanus,
Who loved her, found she had abandoned him.
That was still nothing. Could you ever have claimed
That one day Claudius should prefer you to his son?   1160
It was from Pallas I sought help once more:
Persuaded by him, Claudius adopted you,
Called you Nero, and before the proper time,
Wanted to give you a share of the supreme power.
Then everyone, remembering the past,   1165
Discovered my plan, already too far advanced;
And then the future disgrace of Britannnicus
Excited the murmurs of his father's friends.
My promises dazzled the eyes of some of them;
Exile delivered me from the more seditious;   1170
Claudius, worn out by my unending complaints,
Himself removed from his son all those whose loyalty,
Long committed to follow his destiny,
Might still reopen a way for him to the throne.
I did more: I chose, among my own people,   1175
Those who were to be his tutors and guides.
For you I appointed men of another stamp:
Men who were held in honour by all Rome.

I disregarded intrigues and trusted repute.
I called from exile and drew from the army   1180
Both this same Seneca and this same Burrhus
Who since . . . For Rome thought much of their virtues.
At the same time, exhausting Claudius' riches,
My hand gave gifts from him in your name.
Shows, distributions, irresistible baits,   1185
Won for you both the people's hearts and the soldiers',
Who besides, remembering their old loyalty,
Saw in you my father Germanicus.
Meanwhile Claudius' life was on the wane.
His eyes, so long shut, opened at the end: 1190
He recognized his mistake. Fearful as he was,
Some murmurs favouring his son escaped him;
Too late, he wanted to collect his friends.
His guards, his palace, and his bed were mine.
I made sure his affection bore no fruit,   1195
And that no one but I heard his last sighs.
I took care, while I seemed to ease his sufferings,
That, dying, he knew nothing of his son's tears.
He died. There were rumours at my expense.
I stopped the news getting about too quickly;   1200
And while Burrhus was going secretly
To make the army swear allegiance to you
And you marched to the camp under my auspices,
The altars in Rome were smoking with sacrifices;
The orders that I gave deceived the people   1205
Who prayed for the prince's recovery while he lay dead.
Then, when the sworn obedience of the legions
Had confirmed your authority in the empire,
Claudius was seen; the people, in astonishment,
Learned that you were the emperor and he was dead.   1210
    That is the true confession I wanted to make to you.
Those are all my crimes. And this is my reward.
    You had hardly begun to enjoy the fruit of all these efforts,
Hardly shown your gratitude for six months,
When, tired of a respect which perhaps embarrassed you,   1215
You chose to pretend that you no longer knew me.
I saw Burrhus and Seneca fan your suspicions,
Giving you lessons in disloyalty,

Delighted to see their pupil outdoing them.
I saw Otho and Senecio, debauched young men,   1220
Who flattered you respectfully in all your pleasures,
Taken into your confidence as favourites;
And when, unable to bear your contempt in silence,
I asked you to explain your many insults
(The only refuge of thwarted ingratitude),   1225
Your only answer was to renew your affronts.
Today I promised Junia to your brother
And both of them count on your mother's choice:
What do you do? Junia, carried off to court,
Becomes in one night the object of your love.   1230
I see Octavia erased from your heart,
About to leave the bed I put her in;
I see Pallas banished, your brother arrested;
You even make an attempt upon my freedom:
Burrhus has the effrontery to lay hands on me.   1235
And when, convicted of so many perfidies,
You should receive me only to expiate them,
It is you who tell me to explain myself!

NERO

I never forget that I owe the empire to you,
And, without wearying yourself by repeating it,   1240
Your kindness, madam, could well be content,
Tranquilly assured of my fidelity.
For these suspicions, these assiduous complaints,
Have made everyone who hears them believe
That in the past (I dare say it, between ourselves)   1245
You have used my name only for your own ends.
'So many honours,' they say, 'so much deference,
Are they really slight rewards for what she has done?
What crime has her son committed, to be so condemned?
Did she crown him so that he would obey her?   1250
Does he hold his power only on her behalf?'
Not that, could I have acquiesced thus far,
I should not have been pleased, madam, to yield
This power you seemed to be crying out for.
But Rome wants a master, not a mistress.   1255
You heard the rumours which my weakness gave rise to.
The senate, every day, and the people, angry

To hear me speak only at your dictation,
Gave out that Claudius, when he died, had left me
Not only his power but his taste for obedience.   1260
You have a hundred times seen the soldiers enraged,
Murmuring as they carried the eagles before you;
Ashamed at the indignity this usage offered
To the heroes whose images the standards bear.
Anyone else would have yielded to their pleas;   1265
But if you are not queen you must complain.
Combining against me with Britannicus,
You reinforce him, bringing in Junia's faction,
And Pallas' hand is in all these intrigues.
And, when I overcome my own uneasiness,   1270
You are still full of anger and of hatred.
You want to show my rival to the army;
The rumour has already reached the camp.

AGRIPPINA

I, make him emperor? And you believe it?
You wretch! Why should I? What claim could I have?   1275
What honours could I hope for at his court?
What rank? If I am not spared in your empire,
If my accusers watch my every step,
If they pursue the mother of their emperor,
What should I do in the midst of a different court?   1280
They would reproach me, not for helpless cries,
Or for intentions suffocated at birth,
But for the crimes committed with your knowledge
And for your benefit; I should be convicted.
You cannot deceive me, I see all your tricks.   1285
You are ungrateful as you always were.
From your earliest years, my care and affection
Met no response, your caresses were pretences.
Nothing could get the better of you, you were hard;
It should have stopped my kindness in its traces.   1290
How unhappy I am! By what fatality
Must all my care make me importunate?
I have only one son. O heavens, hear me!
Have I made any vows except for him?
Remorse or fear or danger could not stop me: 1295
I overcame his scorn, averted my eyes

From the disasters which I knew must come.
I did what I could; you are emperor. Enough!
You have deprived me of my liberty;
Take my life too, if that is what you wish,   1300
And may the people, angered by my death,
Not take from you what has cost me so dear.

NERO

Well then, speak out. What is it you want done?

AGRIPPINA

I want my impudent accusers punished,
The anger of Britannicus appeased,   1305
Junia allowed to choose her own husband,
Both of them free, Pallas left where he is;
You to allow me to see you at any hour;
And that same Burrhus, who has been listening,
Told he must never stop me at your door.   1310

NERO

Yes madam, I will in gratitude inscribe
Your power henceforward upon every heart;
Already I bless this lucky chill between us
For kindling our old friendship once again.
Whatever Pallas has done, I will forget it;   1315
I reconcile myself with Britannicus
And, as for this love which has separated us,
You shall decide, I appoint you our judge.
Go then, bear these glad tidings to my brother.
Guards, you are to obey my mother's orders.   1320

SCENE 3

Nero, Burrhus

BURRHUS

What charming spectacles, my lord, this peace,
This reconciliation will present!
You know whether I have ever spoken against her,
Whether I ever sought to spoil your friendship,
And whether I have deserved your unjust anger.   1325

NERO

   I tell you plainly, I found fault with you,
   Burrhus: I thought you two were in league;
   But her hostility makes me trust you again.
   My mother is too quick to triumph, Burrhus:
   I embrace my rival, but it is to choke him.   1330

BURRHUS

   My lord!

NERO

            This is too much. Once and for all,
   He must die, to rid me of Agrippina's fits.
   While he breathes I am only half alive.
   She has made me weary of that hated name;
   I have no mind to suffer her audacity   1335
   Promising him my place a second time.

BURRHUS

   So she is soon to mourn Britannicus?

NERO

   Before this day ends I shall fear him no more.

BURRHUS

   And what leads you to favour such a plan?

NERO

   My glory, my love, my safety, and my life.   1340

BURRHUS

   No, no, say what you will, this foul design
   Was never, my lord, of your own invention.

NERO

   Burrhus!

BURRHUS

           Do I hear this from your own lips?
   And can you hear yourself without a shudder?
   Have you thought what blood this is you mean to wade in? 1345
   Is Nero tired of reigning in all hearts?
   What will they say of you? What are you thinking of?

NERO

   What! would you then have me content myself
   With any chance love that comes and goes in a night,
   Merely to keep my glorious reputation?   1350

Am I to submit to everyone's wishes
Except my own, be emperor just to please them?
BURRHUS
And my lord, to consult your own wishes,
Is it not enough to embrace the public good?
It is for you to choose, you are still the master.   1355
You have been virtuous, you can always be so.
The way is clear, nothing now holds you back:
You have only to go on from virtue to virtue.
But, if you follow the principles of your flatterers,
You will, my lord, be driven from crime to crime,   1360
Backing up your severities with other cruelties,
And dip your hands more deeply still in blood.
The death of Britannicus will excite the zeal
Of friends ready to take up his quarrel.
These avengers too will find defenders   1365
Who, after their death, will find successors.
You are lighting a fire which cannot be put out.
Feared by the whole world, you will have all to fear;
Forever punishing, you will never be safe,
But regard all your subjects as your enemies.   1370
Ah! does the happy experience of your first years
Make you, my lord, hate your innocence?
Do you think of the happiness which distinguished them?
In what quiet, O heavens, those years have passed!
What pleasure to reflect on them, to tell yourself: 1375
'Everywhere, at this moment, I am blessed and loved;
The people do not start when they hear my name;
Heaven does not hear my name among their tears;
No hostile looks follow my appearances,
I see all hearts the lighter as I go by!'   1380
Such were your pleasures. What a change, O gods!
The meanest blood was precious to you once.
One day, as I recall, the senate justly
Asked you to sign a guilty man's death warrant.
My lord, you resisted that severity: 1385
Your heart accused itself of too much cruelty;
You complained of the sorrows inseparable from power:
'I wish', you used to say, 'I could not write.'
No, either believe what I say, or else my death

Shall spare my eyes the pain of this disaster.   1390
I will not be seen to survive your glory,
If you are intent upon so black an action.

[He throws himself on his knees.]

You see me ready, my lord: before you go,
Let my heart be pierced, for it can never consent.
Call those cruel men who have put you up to this;   1395
Let them come and try their yet unpractised hands.
But I see that my tears touch my emperor,
I see that his virtue shudders at their fury.
Lose no time, only name the traitors
Who dare to give you these parricide counsels.   1400
Call your brother, forget in his embrace . . .

NERO

Ah, what are you asking?

BURRHUS

                              No, he does not hate you,
My lord, he is betrayed; I know he is innocent;
I will answer to you for his obedience.
I will go now to speed the happy meeting.   1405

NERO

Let him wait for me in my apartment, with you.

SCENE 4

Nero, Narcissus

NARCISSUS

My lord, I have provided everything
Required for this just death. The poison is ready.
The famous Locusta has excelled herself:
She made a slave die before my eyes;   1410
And steel is less quick to cut off a life
Than the new poison she has entrusted to me.

NERO

Narcissus, that is enough; you have done well,
But I do not wish you to go further.

NARCISSUS

    What! your hatred for Britannicus has weakened   1415
    So that I must . . .

NERO

                Yes, we are to be reconciled.

NARCISSUS

    I would not venture to dissuade you, my lord;
    But he has only just been imprisoned:
    This offence will be fresh in his heart for a long time.
    There are no secrets time does not reveal: 1420
    He will know that my hand was to administer
    A poison which was prepared on your orders.
    May the gods take his mind off this enterprise!
    Yet perhaps, my lord, he will do what you did not dare.

NERO

    His feelings are friendly, they say; I will overcome mine.   1425

NARCISSUS

    And the marriage of Junia is to be the tie?
    My lord, are you making this sacrifice for him?

NERO

    It is not worth the trouble. Be it as it may,
    Narcissus, he is no longer an enemy.

NARCISSUS

    Agrippina, my lord, had promised herself   1430
    She would take control again, and so she has.

NERO

    What? What did she say? And what do you mean?

NARCISSUS

    She boasted about it more or less in public.

NERO

    About what?

NARCISSUS

              That she had only to speak to you,
    After which all these scenes, this fatal anger   1435
    Would give way to the most diffident silence;
    That you would be the first to sign the peace,
    Happy that she deigned to forget everything.

NERO

    But, Narcissus, what would you have me do?
    I am only too inclined to punish his impudence;   1440
    And, so it seems to me, this reckless triumph
    But what would all the world say about it?
    Would soon be punished by eternal regret.
    Do you want me to follow the tyrants' path,
    So that Rome, erasing all its honours,   1445
    Leaves me with only the title of poisoner?
    They will count my revenge an act of parricide.

NARCISSUS

    And, my lord, will you be guided by their whims?
    Did you ever claim that they would always be silent?
    Is it for you to listen to what they say?   1450
    And will you never think of your own desires?
    Will you be the only one you will never credit?
    But, my lord, you do not know the Romans.
    No, no, they are more discreet in what they say.
    So much caution is weakening your reign: 1455
    They will imagine that they should be feared.
    They have long since grown accustomed to the yoke,
    And worship the hand which holds them in its power.
    You will always see them eager to please you.
    Their servility is such that Tiberius grew tired of it.   1460
    Even I, tricked out in a borrowed authority
    Which I received from Claudius when he freed me,
    I have a hundred times, in my days of power,
    Tried their patience, and it has never failed.
    Are you afraid because poison is an atrocity?   1465
    Let the brother die, and then desert the sister:
    Rome, piling the victims upon her altars,
    Though they were innocent would find crimes for them.
    You will see new unlucky days in the calendar:
    Those when the sister and the brother were born.   1470

NERO

    Narcissus, once again, I cannot do it.
    I promised Burrhus, I had to yield to him.
    I do not want to give him, virtuous as he is,
    Arms against me, by not keeping my word.

Useless to set my courage against his reasons;   1475
I cannot listen with an easy mind.

NARCISSUS

Burrhus does not believe all he says,
My lord, he looks to his reputation;
Or rather, all of them have a single thought:
If you do this, they would see their power reduced;   1480
You would be free then, my lord, these masters,
So proud once, would give way like the rest of us.
What! do you not know what they are saying?
'Nero, if they are to be credited,
Was not born for the empire; all he says   1485
And all he does, is what others prescribe for him:
Burrhus directs his heart, Seneca his head.
His only ambition and his special talent
Is driving the winner in a chariot race,
Competing for prizes which are beneath his notice,   1490
Making himself a spectacle to the Romans,
Throwing his voice away upon the stage,
Reciting poems he wants thought masterpieces,
While soldiers are there to make sure the crowd
Will all the time bellow out its applause.'   1495
Ah! do you not want to make them hold their tongues?

NERO

Come, Narcissus. Let's see what we should do.

ACT V

SCENE 1

Britannicus, Junia

BRITANNICUS

Yes, madam, Nero (who would have believed it?)
Is waiting for me now with open arms.
He has invited all the youth of his court.   1500
He wants a great occasion to delight them,
To show that both of us mean what we say
And make our reconciliation the warmer.
He has done with this love which caused such hatred
And leaves you as the sole judge of my fate.   1505
For me, though my ancestral rank is lost
And he decks himself out with it instead,
Since he no longer stands in the way of my love
But seems to leave me the glory of pleasing you,
My heart, I will confess, secretly pardons him,   1510
And the less regrets leaving the rest to him.
So, no more separation from your charms!
So, at this very moment, I can delight in
Those eyes which neither sighs nor terrors moved,
Which gave up empire and emperor for my sake!   1515
Ah, madam! . . . But now, what is this new fear
Which constrains your joy when I am so happy?
Why as you listen do your eyes, sad eyes,
So fixedly turn upwards to the heavens?
What is it that you fear?

JUNIA
                                    I do not know,   1520
And yet, I am afraid.

BRITANNICUS
                        You do love me?

JUNIA
Ah, do I love you!

BRITANNICUS
> Nero, I say,
> No longer sets a barrier to our happiness.

JUNIA
> But can you promise me he is sincere?

BRITANNICUS
> What! You suspect his hate goes on in secret?   1525

JUNIA
> Just now Nero loved me and swore to finish you.
> He is abandoning me and seeking your friendship.
> My lord, can such a change happen suddenly?

BRITANNICUS
> Agrippina, madam, has brought this about.
> She thought my ruin would be the end of her.   1530
> Thanks to the jealous fears she entertains,
> Our greatest enemies are now our friends.
> I rely on her passionate manner with me;
> I rely on Burrhus; I even believe his master:
> I think that like me, he cannot be treacherous;   1535
> Either he hates openly, or not at all.

JUNIA
> My lord, you should not judge his heart by yours:
> For you and he proceed in different ways.
> Nero and Nero's court are new to me;
> But, in this single day of my acquaintance,   1540
> How far apart have been their words and thoughts!
> How little at one, it seems, are lips and hearts!
> What pleasure people take in treachery!
> It is a foreign land for you and me!

BRITANNICUS
> But, whether his friendship is real or pretended,   1545
> You may fear Nero, but has he no fear?
> No, no, he will not, by some cowardly outrage,
> Set people and senate up in arms against him.
> What am I saying? He knows he has been unjust.
> Even Narcissus saw that he was sorry.   1550
> Ah, if, princess, he had told you how far . . .

JUNIA
> But Narcissus, my lord, is he not betraying you?

BRITANNICUS

And what makes you think I should not trust him?

JUNIA

What do I know? My lord, your life is at stake.
I suspect everything. Nothing is safe;   1555
I fear Nero, I fear my constant misfortune.
Filled with a black foreboding, in spite of myself
I fear even to let you out of my sight.
Alas, suppose this peace you make so much of
Should yet conceal some trap to take your life!   1560
Suppose Nero, provoked by our common purpose,
Had chosen the night to hide his revenge!
Suppose he was so occupied now, while I see you,
And I am talking to you for the last time!
Ah, prince!

BRITANNICUS

           You are crying! Ah, my dear princess!   1565
And your heart feels for me to that point!
What, madam! on a day when, full of his greatness,
Nero thinks he will dazzle you with his splendour,
In this place where I am avoided and he is worshipped,
You prefer my wretched condition to his pomp,   1570
And this very day and in this very place
Refuse an empire, and weep before my eyes!
But, madam, cease to shed these precious tears;
I will return soon to allay your fears.
Longer delay could only make me suspect.   1575
Goodbye, I am going, my heart full of love,
Amidst the blind enthusiasm of youth,
To see, to think, only of my lovely princess.
Goodbye.

JUNIA

           Prince...

BRITANNICUS

           They are waiting, I must go.

JUNIA

But at least wait until they send for you.   1580

SCENE 2

Agrippina, Britannicus, Junia

AGRIPPINA

    Prince, why are you late? You must go at once.
    Nero is complaining impatiently of your absence.
    The guests are all assembled, full of joy,
    Which will break out the moment you are reconciled.
    Do not let the moment pass; they are right to long for it.   1585
    Go. And we, madam, will go to see Octavia.

BRITANNICUS

    Go, lovely Junia, and with your mind at rest
    Speedily embrace my sister, she awaits you.
    As soon as I can, I will come back to you,
    Madam, and thank you for all you have done.   1590

SCENE 3

Agrippina, Junia

AGRIPPINA

    Madam, unless I am mistaken, some tears
    Fell and clouded your eyes as you said goodbye.
    May I know what is troubling you? Is it possible
    You suspect this peace which is my handiwork?

JUNIA

    After all the trouble which this day has brought,   1595
    Could I calm the agitation of my spirits?
    Alas! I still hardly believe this miracle.
    Even though I feared some obstacle to your kindnesses,
    Change, madam, is common enough at court;
    And love can never be quite free of fear.   1600

AGRIPPINA

    Enough. I have spoken, everything has changed:
    What I have done leaves no place for suspicions.
    I will answer for this peace so solemnly promised me;
    Nero has given me pledges not to be doubted.

Ah! Had you seen how tenderly he caressed me   1605
As he renewed the promises he had made!
How we embraced! Just now he stopped me leaving;
His arms, as we said goodbye, would hardly let go!
His openness and kindness shone in his face.
He told me all, down to his smallest secrets.   1610
He poured out his heart like a son, voluntarily,
Forgetting his pride, in his mother's arms.
But then, resuming a severe countenance,
He was the emperor consulting his mother;
With sublime confidence he put in my hands   1615
Secrets on which the fate of nations depends.
No, to his glory it must here be said
That in his heart there is no deadly malice;
And only our enemies made him less kind,
Exploiting his easy ways, to damage us.   1620
But now their power in turn is declining.
Rome will know Agrippina once again:
Already they love the rumour that I am back.
But let us not wait for nightfall here.
Let us go to Octavia's, and give her what remains   1625
Of a day as happy as I thought it fatal.
But what is that I hear? There is some disturbance.
What can be happening?

JUNIA

> Heaven, save Britannicus!

SCENE 4

Agrippina, Junia, Burrhus

AGRIPPINA
Burrhus, why are you running? Stop, what was that...?

BURRHUS
Madam, it is done. Britannicus is dying.   1630

JUNIA
Ah, my prince!

AGRIPPINA

> He is dying?

BURRHUS

      He is dead,
Madam.

JUNIA

    Forgive me, madam, the discourtesy,
I'm going to help him, if I can, or follow him.

SCENE 5

Agrippina, Burrhus

AGRIPPINA

 What an outrage, Burrhus!

BURRHUS

       It is my end too,
Madam: I must leave the court and the emperor.   1635

AGRIPPINA

 What! Did he not shrink from his brother's blood?

BURRHUS

 The plot was carried out less openly.
 The emperor had hardly seen his brother arrive;
 He rose, embraced him, there was silence; suddenly
 Caesar first took a cup in his own hand: 1640
 'To end this day with better auspices,
 My hand pours the first-fruits from this cup,'
 He said; 'You gods, whom I thus invoke,
 Come and look favourably on our reunion.'
 Britannicus bound himself by the same vows;   1645
 The cup in his hand was filled by Narcissus;
 His lips, however, had hardly touched the rim,
 A sword could not have worked more suddenly,
 Madam: the light was snatched from his eyes;
 He fell upon his couch lifeless and cold.   1650
 Imagine how this shock struck everyone:
 Half of those present, stunned, cried out and left;
 But those who knew the court better, stayed
 And, watching Caesar's face, mended their looks.
 Meanwhile, he remained bending over the couch; 1655
 He showed no trace of astonishment:

'This attack,' he said, 'which seems so violent,
He often suffered in childhood, without danger.'
Narcissus tried in vain to look troubled;
The traitor could not help showing his joy.   1660
As for me, whatever the emperor might do to me,
I made my way through the crowd in this odious court;
And I went, crushed by this assassination,
To mourn Britannicus, Caesar, and the whole state.

AGRIPPINA

Here he is. You will see whether I put him up to it.   1665

SCENE 6

Agrippina, Nero, Burrhus, Narcissus

NERO, *seeing Agrippina.*
  Gods!

AGRIPPINA
      Stop, Nero: I must have a word with you.
Britannicus is dead, I know what happened;
I know the assassin.

NERO
              Who then, madam?

AGRIPPINA
                  You.

NERO
I! So you suspect me of everything.
No trouble comes but I am held responsible;   1670
If one were to listen, madam, to what you say,
It was my hand which put an end to Claudius.
You loved his son: his death may be a shock,
But I cannot answer for the bolts of fate.

AGRIPPINA
No, no, Britannicus has died of poison: 1675
Narcissus did it and you ordered it.

NERO
Madam, what makes you say such things?

NARCISSUS
                  My lord,

Does this suspicion seem so outrageous?
Britannicus, madam, had secret designs
Which would have given you cause for regret.   1680
He aimed at more than marriage with Junia:
He would have punished you for your kindness to him.
He was deceiving you; he was offended;
Sooner or later he would have recalled the past.
So, whether fate, in spite of you, has served you,   1685
Or whether, knowing the plots against his life,
Caesar saw fit to trust my loyalty,
Let your enemies weep, madam, but no one else.
They may consider this the worst of ills,
But you . . .

AGRIPPINA
              Nero, persist with such ministers.   1690
You will be able to boast of some glorious deeds.
You did not take this step to shrink in future.
Your hand has begun with your brother's blood;
I can see you will go on to strike your mother.
I know that in your heart of hearts you hate me;   1695
You will want to rid yourself of my assistance.
But I intend that my death shall do you no good.
Do not suppose I shall leave you alone when I die.
Rome, this heaven, this light you owe to me,
Will everywhere keep me before your eyes.   1700
Your remorse will follow you like all the Furies;
You will try to calm it by other atrocities;
Your madness will grow worse as you go on,
Will stain your every day with some fresh blood.
But I hope that heaven at last, tired of your crimes,   1705
Will add your death to all those other victims;
That, after covering yourself with their blood and mine,
You will find yourself compelled to shed your own;
And your name will be such that, to posterity,
The cruellest tyrants will think it an insult.   1710
    That is what my heart prophesies for you.
Goodbye: you may go now.

NERO
                      Narcissus, follow me.

SCENE 7

Agrippina, Burrhus

AGRIPPINA

Ah, how unjust my suspicions were!
I condemned Burrhus and listened to Narcissus.
Burrhus, did you see what furious looks   1715
Nero gave me by way of farewell?
That is it: nothing can stop him now;
The predicted blow will fall upon my head.
He will crush you also, in your turn.

BURRHUS

Ah, madam, I have lived a day too long.   1720
Would to heaven his cruel hand had fortunately
Tried out its new fury upon me!
That he had not given me, by this murder,
Too sure a pledge of troubles for the State!
It is not his crime alone which kills my hopes;   1725
Jealousy could have armed him against his brother;
To tell you, madam, truthfully why I grieve:
Nero watched him die without changing colour.
The indifference which shows in his eyes
Is that of a tyrant hardened to crime from childhood.   1730
Let him finish, madam, and have put to death
An importunate minister whom he cannot bear.
I have no wish now to escape his anger;
To me the quickest death would be the best.

SCENE 8

Agrippina, Burrhus, Albina

ALBINA

Ah! madam, ah! my lord, run to the emperor: 1735
Come and save Caesar from his own fury.
He finds himself separated for ever from Junia.

AGRIPPINA

What? Has Junia ended her own life?

ALBINA
   To trouble Caesar to eternity,
   Madam, without dying she has died for him.   1740
   You know how she made her escape from here:
   She then pretended to go to poor Octavia;
   But soon she took passages and back ways
   Where my eyes followed her precipitous steps.
   She went out of the palace gates wildly.   1745
   First she caught sight of Augustus' statue;
   And making the feet of it wet with her tears
   She threw her arms around them and hugged them:
   Then she said: 'Prince, by these knees I hold,
   Protect now what is left of your race.   1750
   Rome has just seen sacrificed in your palace
   The only surviving prince who resembled you.
   They want me to betray him after his death;
   But, always to keep my faith to him pure,
   Prince, I vow myself to the deathless gods   1755
   Whose altars, through your virtues, you now share.'
   Meanwhile the populace, amazed at the sight,
   Darted from all sides and crowded round her,
   Touched by her tears; and, pitying her trouble,
   With one voice declared they would protect her.   1760
   They led her to the temple, where so long
   Our dedicated virgins have served religiously,
   Faithfully keeping alive their precious charge,
   The flame which always burns there for our gods.
   Caesar saw them go and dared not interfere.   1765
   Narcissus, bolder, rushed to do his will.
   He sped towards Junia, and without scruple
   Began to lay a profane hand upon her.
   A thousand mortal blows punished his zeal;
   His treacherous blood bespattered Junia.   1770
   Caesar, struck by so many things at once,
   Left him in the hands of those who surrounded him.
   He came back. Now, no one dares approach him,
   So wild and silent is he. The name of Junia
   Is now the only sound to pass his lips.   1775
   He moves at random; his uncertain eyes
   Wander but dare not look up to heaven;

People fear that if night and solitude
Render his restless despair more bitter still,
If you leave him longer without assistance,   1780
In his grief, he may try to kill himself.
Time is short: hurry. It needs only a whim,
He would destroy himself, madam.

AGRIPPINA

                              So he should.
But, Burrhus, let us see where his rage is taking him,
What alteration his remorse will bring,   1785
Whether he will act differently in future.

BURRHUS

Would to the gods this were the last of his crimes!

PHAEDRA

tragedy

1677

HERE is another tragedy the subject of which is taken from Euripides. Although I have followed a slightly different route from that of this author, in the conduct of the plot, I have not failed to embellish my play with everything which seemed to me most striking in his. Even if I owed him only the idea of the character of Phaedra, I could say that I owe what is perhaps the most reasonable matter I have put on the stage. It does not surprise me at all that this character should have had so great a success in the time of Euripides, and that it also succeeded so well in our own age, because it has all the qualities which Aristotle requires in a tragic hero, and which are capable of exciting pity and terror. Phaedra is, actually, neither altogether guilty nor altogether innocent. She is committed by her fate, and by the wrath of the gods, to an illicit love, the horror of which she is the first to feel. She makes every effort to overcome it. She would rather die than admit it to anyone. And when she is forced to reveal it, she speaks of it in a confusion which makes it clear that her crime is a punishment from the gods rather than a motion of her own will.

I have even taken care to make her rather less odious than she is in the classical tragedies, in which she decides on her own to accuse Hippolytus. I thought that the calumny was something too base and too dark to put in the mouth of a princess who otherwise has such noble and virtuous feelings. This baseness appeared to me more appropriate to a nurse, who might have more servile inclinations, and who none the less undertakes this false accusation only to save the life and honour of her mistress. Phaedra involves herself in it only because she is in an agitation of mind which makes her beside herself, and immediately afterwards she thinks of justifying innocence and declaring the truth.

Hippolytus is accused, in Euripides and in Seneca, of having actually raped his stepmother: 'He took her by force.' But here he is accused only of having had the intention of doing so. I wished to spare Theseus a confusion which might perhaps have made him less agreeable to the audience.

As to the character of Hippolytus, I have observed that in

classical times Euripides was blamed for having shown him as a
philosopher free of all imperfections: which had the effect that
the death of this young prince gave rise much more to indignation
than to pity. I thought I should give him some weakness which
would make him slightly culpable towards his father, without
however detracting from the greatness of soul which leads him
to spare Phaedra's honour, and to allow himself to be oppressed
without accusing her. What I call weakness is the passion which,
in spite of himself, he feels for Aricia, who is the daughter and
the sister of his father's mortal enemies.

This Aricia is not a character I have invented. Virgil says that
Hippolytus married her and had a daughter by her, after
Aesculapius had brought him back to life. I have also read in some
authors that Hippolytus had married and taken to Italy a young
Athenian girl of high birth, who was called Aricia, and who had
given her name to a little town in Italy.

I mention these authorities, because I have been scrupulous
about following the legend. I have even followed the history of
Theseus, as it is in Plutarch.

It is in this historian that I found that what gave occasion for
the belief that Theseus descended into the underworld to carry off
Proserpine was a journey this prince made in Epirus, towards the
source of Acheron, to visit a king whose wife Pirithous wanted
to carry off, and who kept Theseus prisoner, after having put
Pirithous to death. In this way I have tried to preserve the probability of the history, without detracting from the attractions of
the legend, which contribute greatly to the poetry. And the
rumour of Theseus' death, founded on this fabulous journey, gives
Phaedra occasion to make a declaration of love which becomes
one of the chief causes of her misfortune, and which she would
never have dared to make as long as she had believed that her
husband was alive.

For the rest, I do not yet dare to assert that this play is actually
the best of my tragedies. I leave it to readers and to time to decide
as to its true value. What I can assert is that I have written
none in which virtue is shown in a clearer light than it is here.
The smallest faults are severely punished in it. The mere thought
of crime is regarded with as much horror as the crime itself. The
weaknesses of love are treated in it as real weaknesses; passions
are presented to view only to show all the confusion they cause;

and vice is everywhere painted in such colours as to make its ugliness known and hated. That is the aim which everyone who works for public consumption ought to have in mind; and this is what the first tragic poets had in mind above everything. Their theatre is a school in which virtue was taught no less than in the schools of the philosophers. And so Aristotle laid down rules for the dramatic poem; and Socrates, the wisest of philosophers, was not above giving a hand with the tragedies of Euripides. One could wish that our works were as solid and as full of useful teaching as those of these poets. It would perhaps be a way of bringing to a reconciliation with tragedy a number of people, celebrated for their piety and their doctrine, who in recent times have condemned it, people who would no doubt judge of it more favourably if the authors thought as much about instructing their audiences as about entertaining them, and if in that way they followed the true purpose of tragedy.

THE CHARACTERS

THESEUS, son of Aegeus, king of Athens

PHAEDRA, wife of Theseus, daughter of Minos and Pasiphaë

HIPPOLYTUS, son of Theseus and of Antiope, queen of the
  Amazons

THERAMENES, tutor to Hippolytus

ARICIA, a princess of the royal house of Athens

OENONE, nurse and confidante to Phaedra

ISMENE, confidante to Aricia

PANOPE, one of Phaedra's waiting-women

Guards

The scene is in Troezene, a town in the Peloponnese.

ACT I

SCENE 1

Hippolytus, Theramenes

HIPPOLYTUS
It is decided. I will go from here,
Leave this agreeable shore, Theramenes,
And leave Troezene. With everything in doubt
I am ashamed to be doing nothing.
It is six months since I saw my father,   5
I do not know what has befallen him,
Nor even where his dear head may lie.

THERAMENES
Where then, sir, are you going to look for him?
In an attempt to pacify your fears
I have scoured the seas on both sides of Corinth;   10
Asked after Theseus upon those shores
Where Acheron disappears among the dead;*
I have been to Elis and, passing Tenaros,
Visited the sea into which Icarus fell.*
What fresh hope have you, in what happy lands   15
Do you expect to find a trace of him?
Who knows, can we be sure the king your father
Wants us to know the secret of his absence?
May it not be that, while we fear for him,
He's calmly hiding some new love from us   20
And waiting for some unfortunate girl to . . .

HIPPOLYTUS
Enough of that, Theramenes, and speak
Respectfully of Theseus! There were errors,
Certainly, in his youth, but for the future
We can be sure he will not err again;   25
Phaedra has long settled his affections
And has no fear of any rivals now.
So I shall look for him, it is my duty,
This place is now impossible, I shall leave.

THERAMENES
    How long, sir, have you been afraid to stay   30
    In this place where everything is so peaceful
    And where you were so happy as a child;
    Where I have seen you better pleased to be
    Than in the splendour of the court at Athens?
    What danger or what trouble drives you out?   35

HIPPOLYTUS
    That happy time has gone and all has changed
    Since the gods sent upon this coast of ours
    The daughter of Minos and Pasiphaë.*

THERAMENES
    I understand. The cause of your distress
    Is known to me; that Phaedra should be here   40
    Troubles you and the sight of her is wounding.
    A dangerous stepmother, her influence showed
    The moment that she set her eyes on you
    And without more ado she had you exiled.
    But now her hatred's gone or has grown less.   45
    Besides, how can a woman who is dying
    And wants to die, be any threat to you?
    Phaedra is suffering and will not say why;
    Tired of herself and of the air she breathes,
    Can she plot anything against you now?   50

HIPPOLYTUS
    It is not her hostility I fear.
    I leave her to escape another enemy.
    I am escaping from the young Aricia,
    Last of a race sworn to our destruction.

THERAMENES
    But, sir, you are not persecuting her?   55
    Did this young lady, though she was the sister
    Of the cruel sons of Pallas, ever meddle
    With the designs of her perfidious brothers?
    Should you hate her? Her charms are innocent.

HIPPOLYTUS
    If I hated her I would not run away.   60

THERAMENES

Sir, may I guess the reason for your flight?
Can it be that the proud Hippolytus,
Implacable against the laws of love
And the yoke Theseus has so often borne,
Is so no longer? Can it be that Venus   65
Wants to show Theseus was right after all?
That she is treating you like other mortals
And forcing you to worship at her shrine.
Could you be in love, sir?

HIPPOLYTUS

                                    How dare you, friend?
You have known me since the day I was born;   70
How can you ask me shamefully to give up
The haughty pride you know is in my heart?
An Amazon was my mother and I sucked*
That pride in with her milk—but that is nothing;
When I arrived at riper years myself   75
I could not but approve the self I found.
You were then my attached and zealous tutor,
Accustomed to recount my father's story.
You knew with what attention I would listen
And how I warmed to all his noble deeds,   80
When you described this intrepid hero
Who consoled men for losing Hercules,*
Told me of monsters strangled, brigands punished,
Procrustes, Cercyon, of Scirron and Sinnis,
The giant's bones scattered at Epidaurus,   85
And all Crete reeking of the Minotaur's blood.
But, when you touched upon less glorious deeds,
His troth plighted in a hundred places,
Helen in Sparta stolen from her parents,*
Salamis witnessing Periboea's tears,   90
So many others, whose names he forgot,
Too credulous, betrayed by his flame;
As Ariadne, complaining to the rocks;
Phaedra too taken, under better auspices;
You know with what regret I heard such talk,   95
Begging you many times to cut it short.
Happy had I been able to erase

The unworthy half of this fine history!
And is it now my turn to be so bound?
And would the gods so far have humbled me,   100
The more contemptible in my weak sighs
In that while Theseus might be excused
For all the heap of honours he has earned
I cannot claim I have tamed any monsters
Which might give me the right to fail like him.   105
Even suppose my pride had been diminished
Should I have chosen Aricia as the instrument?
My straying senses could not but remember
The obstacle which stands between us two.
My father disapproves of her and prohibits   110
A union that would give his brother nephews:
He fears a shoot sprung from a guilty stock
And wants the name extinguished with their sister;
She is to be his ward until she dies
And in the meantime she is not to marry.   115
Should I take sides with her against my father?
Is it for me to set such an example?
And my youth, launched upon a reckless love . . .

THERAMENES
Ah, but if once your hour has struck, my lord,
Heaven will not give a thought to our reasons.   120
Theseus, trying to close your eyes, has opened them;
His hatred fans the flame of rebellion
And gives fresh graces to his enemy.
So why resist an innocent affection?
If it has charms, why not give way to it?   125
Is a wild scruple always to be followed?
Hercules strayed, and should you fear to do so?
Who has not in the end been tamed by Venus?
Where would you be yourself, you who resist her,
If Antiope had not relented,   130
Consumed by a chaste love for Theseus?
But does all this proud talk serve any purpose?
Admit it, everything's different; these last days
You have not been the same Hippolytus,
The wild and unapproachable young man   135
Driving a chariot along the shore

Or, expert in the art Neptune invented,
Boldly riding a stallion from the herd.
We have not been hallooing in the woods,
A hidden fire has made your eyes less keen. 140
No doubt about it, you must be in love:
You're pining and you will not tell us why.
Can it be that you find Aricia charming?

HIPPOLYTUS

Theramenes, I'm off to find my father.

THERAMENES

Will you not see Phaedra before you go, 145
My lord?

HIPPOLYTUS

       Of course, let her know I am coming.
We'll see her, for I must be dutiful.
But here comes the queen's dear Oenone;
What fresh misfortune is disturbing her?

SCENE 2

Hippolytus, Oenone, Theramenes

OENONE

Who has more reason than I to be disturbed? 150
Oh my lord, the queen is on her death-bed.
Night and day I spend myself watching her;
She is dying in my arms and will not say why.
Her mind is eternally in disorder.
Her bed cannot hold her in her restless grief. 155
She must be in the light; in her great pain
She will have me keep everyone away ...
She's coming.

HIPPOLYTUS

       That's it. I must be off
So that she does not see a face she hates.

SCENE 3

Phaedra, Oenone

PHAEDRA

Let's go no further, but stop here, Oenone.   160
I cannot manage for my strength has gone;
Seeing the light again dazzles my eyes
And my knees tremble and are giving way.
Oh dear!   [She sits down.]

OENONE

Almighty gods, may our tears appease you!   165

PHAEDRA

How heavy they seem, these ornaments, these veils!
Whose hand, unasked, has tied up all these knots,
Has carefully set my hair about my forehead?
Everything hurts and conspires to do me harm.

OENONE

How your wishes conflict with one another!   170
It was you who, a little while ago,
Denounced your own intentions as unjust
And urged me to put all your finery on;
It was you, with your former strength in mind,
Who wanted to be seen, and see the light: 175
You see it, ma'am, and now you want to hide;
Do you now hate the light you were looking for?

PHAEDRA

Noble and brilliant author of a sad family,
You whose daughter my mother dared claim to be,
Who perhaps redden with shame at my distress,   180
O Sun, this is the last time I shall see you!

OENONE

What! you still entertain that cruel longing?
Must I still see you giving up hope of life?
Is it for death you make these preparations?

PHAEDRA

Gods! if I could rest in a dark forest!   185
When shall I, through a cloud of noble dust,
Watch a chariot disappear in the distance?

OENONE

    What, ma'am?

PHAEDRA

              I am mad! Oh, where am I?
    What have I said? My mind is wandering.
    Gone then! the gods have left me desolate.   190
    Oenone, my face is covered with blushes;
    You can see what I suffer from too clearly;
    Do what I will, my eyes fill with tears.

OENONE

    If you must blush, blush because you are silent
    And so exacerbate your violent ills.   195
    Must you refuse our care, be deaf to our words
    And proceed pitilessly to your death?
    What fury stops your life in mid-course?
    What spell or poison has dried up its spring?
    Three times darkness has overspread the sky   200
    Since last your eyes admitted trace of sleep,
    And day has three times chased off the dark night
    Since any food entered your weakened body.
    I beg you, do not let yourself be tempted:
    What right have you to try to kill yourself?   205
    You offend the gods from whom your life proceeds;
    You betray the husband to whom you gave your word;
    You betray your children to a long unhappiness
    Under a tutelage which must be rigorous.
    Consider, on the day they lose their mother   210
    The foreigner's son will be given fresh hope,
    Your proud enemy, the enemy of your race,
    This son once carried in an Amazon's womb,
    Hippolytus, this . . .

PHAEDRA

              Gods!

OENONE

                That gives you pause?

PHAEDRA

    Unhappy woman, what name have you uttered?   215

OENONE

Ah, now you have reason to be angry.
I like to see you shudder at that name.
Then live. Let love and duty have their way.
Live and you will not let a Scythian's son
Assume a crushing sway over your children, 220
The best blood of Greece and of the gods.
But do not let time pass, for time is mortal.
Recruit your wasted strength, do it at once
While there is still a flicker of life in you;
Fan it at least, before it goes out. 225

PHAEDRA

My fault is, I have lived too long already.

OENONE

Is it remorse tearing you apart?
What crime can make it so unrelenting?
Your hands have not dabbled in innocent blood.

PHAEDRA

Thank heaven, my hands are not criminal. 230
If only my heart were as innocent!

OENONE

What project did you form within yourself
So frightful that your heart is still terrified?

PHAEDRA

I have said enough already. Spare me now.
I am dying because to confess would be death. 235

OENONE

Then die, persist in your inhuman silence,
But look for someone else to close your eyes.
Although your flickering life is almost done,
My spirit will be first among the dead
Who always beckon us a thousand ways; 240
My grief entitles me to take the shortest.
You are so cruel! When have you found me fail you?
I left country and children for your sake.
Is this how you reward my devotion?

PHAEDRA

Why be so violent? What good will it do? 245
It will appal you if I break my silence.

OENONE

     Great gods, can anything you have to say
     Be worse than you dying before my eyes?

PHAEDRA

     If I confessed my crime, and if you knew
     What lot the Fates have meted out to me,   250
     I should still die, and die more culpable.

OENONE

     I beg you by the tears I shed for you,
     And by the feeble limbs that I embrace,
     Deliver my mind from this fatal doubt.

PHAEDRA

     It is your wish: get up.

OENONE

                Speak, I am listening.   255

PHAEDRA

     What can I say to her, heavens? How begin?

OENONE

     It is your terrors which affront me most.

PHAEDRA

     Venus hates me! Her anger is fatal!
     To what confusions did love lead my mother!

OENONE

     Let us not think of them, ma'am: for the future   260
     Eternal silence cover the remembrance.

PHAEDRA

     My sister Ariadne, you were caught*
     And died where Theseus had abandoned you!

OENONE

     What is it, ma'am? What disturbs you so,
     Setting you against your own flesh and blood?   265

PHAEDRA

     I am the last of that deplorable race;
     Since Venus wishes it, I die the last of them
     And the unhappiest.

OENONE

               Are you in love?

PHAEDRA
    I suffer all the furies love can bring.

OENONE
    For whom?

PHAEDRA
                    Now you will hear the full horror.   270
    I love . . . I tremble and shiver at the name.
    I love . . .

OENONE
            Who?

PHAEDRA
                    You know the Amazon's son,
    This prince I have for so long oppressed.

OENONE
    Hippolytus! Great gods!

PHAEDRA
                            It was you named him.

OENONE
    Just heavens! All my blood runs cold, it freezes.   275
    Despair! Crime! A deplorable race!
    Why did we come here? Shores of ill omen,
    Were we obliged to make this fatal journey?

PHAEDRA
    My trouble comes from further back. No sooner
    Had I become the wife of Theseus,   280
    Contentment, happiness seemed well assured,
    Then Athens showed me my proud enemy.
    I saw him: I blushed and grew pale seeing him;
    Then in my mind, what turbulence arose!
    My eyes were blinded and I could not speak;   285
    I felt my whole body grow hot and cold.
    I recognized the terrible fires of Venus,
    Torments inevitable in a race she persecutes.
    I was assiduous in all the vows
    I thought would placate and deflect her: 290
    I built a temple to her, decorated it;
    At all times I had victims for sacrifice
    And hoped by stabbing them to find my reason:

That was no remedy for invincible love!
In vain my hand burnt incense at the altars;   295
But all the time my lips implored the goddess,
My adoration was for Hippolytus;
He was always there, even when the altars smoked
It was to him, this god I dared not name,
I offered everything. I avoided him,   300
The worst torture of all! My eyes saw him
Even in the features of his father.
I had the courage to go against myself
And forced myself at last to persecute him.
To banish the enemy I idolized   305
I pretended the injustice of a stepmother;
For ever calling out for his exile,
I tore him from the arms of his father.
I breathed at last, Oenone, once he was absent,
My days were less troubled; they were innocent: 310
I concealed my grief: obedient to my husband
I cosseted the children of our marriage.
My precautions were vain. By cruel fate
My husband himself brought me to Troezene:
The enemy that I had banished was there   315
And my too recent wound began to bleed.
No longer is it a secret fire in my veins;
It is Venus motionless upon her prey.
I have a proper terror of my crime;
I hate life and my love horrifies me;   320
Dying, I wanted to keep my good name
And not let my dark love into the light:
Your tears were too much for me, and you fought me;
I have confessed: I do not regret it
So long as you, seeing me so near death,   325
No longer hurt me with unjust reproaches
And make no further effort to revive
The last faint warmth now ready to depart.

SCENE 4

Phaedra, Oenone, Panope

PANOPE

I have sad news that I should wish to hide
From you, ma'am, but my duty is to tell it.   330
Death has removed your invincible lord
And you alone are not informed of it.

OENONE

What are you saying, Panope?

PANOPE

That the queen
Now prays in vain for Theseus' return,
And that his son Hippolytus has been told   335
By ships just in to port, that he is dead.

PHAEDRA

Heavens!

PANOPE

Athens is divided; one party
Thinks that the prince your son should be king;
The other, ma'am, so far forgets the laws
As to give its suffrage to the foreigner's son.   340
It is even said that an insolent faction
Designs to put Aricia on the throne
And so to let the race of Pallas triumph.
I thought that I should warn you of this danger.
Already Hippolytus is about to go;   345
The fear is that if he shows himself
In the midst of this confusion, all the crowd,
Fickle as usual, will adhere to him.

OENONE

Enough said, Panope. The queen hears you
And she will see the warning is important.   350

SCENE 5

Phaedra, Oenone

OENONE

  Ma'am, my persuasions were at an end,
I was no longer urging you to live
And thought rather of following you to the tomb,
No longer having the heart to keep you from it;
But this fresh trouble calls for other counsels.   355
Your fortune changes and looks different now.
The king has gone, ma'am, you must take his place.
His death leaves you a son to whom you are bound,
A slave if he loses you, if you live, a king.
In his misfortune, to whom can he turn?   360
Where will the hand be that should dry his tears?
His innocent cries, reaching up to heaven,
Will rouse his divine ancestors against you.
Live, you need not reprove yourself further:
Your love becomes an ordinary love,   365
For by his death Theseus has cut the bonds
Which made a crime, a horror, of your passion.
You have less to fear now from Hippolytus;
It is not culpable to see him now.
Convinced of your aversion, it is possible   370
He will consent to lead the sedition.
Put him right, and make his courage falter.
He is king here, Troezene falls to him,
But he knows that the law will give your son
The superb ramparts that Minerva built.*   375
Both of you have a natural enemy:
You should combine against Aricia.

PHAEDRA

  Well, I will let myself be influenced
By your advice and will consent to live,
If anyone can bring me back to life   380
And if love of a son, in this dark moment,
Can revive the poor remnant of my spirits.

ACT II

SCENE 1

Aricia, Ismene

ARICIA

Hippolytus has asked to see me here?
Hippolytus wants to say goodbye to me?
Ismene, are you sure you're not mistaken?   385

ISMENE

It is the death of Theseus has done this.
You must expect such changes everywhere.
Theseus kept people from you: that is over.
At last, madam, you are your own mistress;
The whole of Greece will soon be at your feet.   390

ARICIA

Then it is something more than idle rumour,
Ismene? Am I then no more a slave
And have I really no more enemies?

ISMENE

Madam, the gods are not against you now,
And Theseus is with your brothers' shades.   395

ARICIA

Is it known what adventure caused his death?

ISMENE

The most unlikely tales are told about it.
It is said that he was carrying off some girl
—Another—and the waves swallowed him up.
It is even said—the rumour's everywhere—   400
That he descended to the underworld
With Pirithoüs, that with him he saw*
The melancholy banks of Cocytus*
And showed himself among the infernal shades,
But that he could not find the way back   405
Nor pass those frontiers from which none returns.

ARICIA

Am I to believe that a mortal man,
Before his last hour has come, can penetrate
The profound regions which the dead inhabit?
What charm could draw him to that dreaded land?   410

ISMENE

Theseus is dead, madam, no one else doubts it.
Athens mourns for him, all Troezene knows
And recognizes Hippolytus as king.
Phaedra, here in this palace, fears for her son
And takes counsel with her troubled friends.   415

ARICIA

And you think that, more humane than his father,
Hippolytus will make my lot easier,
Take pity on my misfortunes?

ISMENE

                I do, madam.

ARICIA

Hippolytus has no feelings: do you know him?
On what slight thread do you hang your hopes?   420
He thinks nothing of women; am I so different?
He has kept out of our way for so long,
Preferring places where he will not find us.

ISMENE

I know all the tales about his coldness;
But I have seen Hippolytus in your presence,   425
And I have watched him the more carefully
Because of all this talk about his pride.
With you, he seemed to be a different man,
One look from you and he became confused;
Although his eyes were trying to avoid you   430
They softened and he could not keep them off you.
Perhaps he scorns to be called a lover;
He has the eyes of one, if not the words.

ARICIA

Ismene, my dear, how avidly I listen
To what you say, yet perhaps there's nothing in it!   435
You know me well, did you think it possible

That such a heart as mine, all tears and bitterness
From its earliest days, was after all to know
The follies and the pains of being in love?
Last of my race, the daughter of a king   440
Whose mother was no less than Earth herself,
I was the only one to escape destruction.
I lost, in the first flower of their youth,
Six brothers . . . Could an illustrious house not hope?
The sword took all of them, the earth reluctantly   445
Drank the blood of the nephews of Erechtheus.
You know how, since their death, a severe law
Has made it treason for the Greeks to love me.
The fear is that their sister might revive
The flames concealed in her brothers' ashes.   450
But you know too with what disdainful eye
I looked upon the conqueror's suspicions;
You know I had no appetite for love
And often thanked the unjust Theseus
Whose rigour fitted well with my contempt.   455
My eyes had not then lighted on his son.
Not that I merely gave way to the spell
My eyes submit to when they see his beauty,
Or love him for the grace they talk so much of.
These are the gifts nature has honoured him with,   460
But which he scorns, and seems not to recognize.
I love, I prize in him more noble qualities,
The virtues of his father, not the weaknesses.
I love, I must confess, this generous pride
Which never felt the need to stoop to love.   465
Phaedra was pleased that Theseus wanted her:
I am prouder, and disdain the easy glory
Of tributes offered to a thousand others
And want no place in a heart open to all.
But to make an inflexible courage falter,   470
To give pain to a heart that has no feelings,
To bind a prisoner whom his bonds astonish,
Who resists and yet takes delight in them:
That's what I want, that is what rouses me.
Hercules was harder to disarm   475
Than is Hippolytus; more often conquered,

More quickly overcome, he brought less glory
To the eyes which tamed him. But, dear Ismene,
There will be only too much resistance;
I am imprudent, you will see me humbled,   480
Perhaps bemoaning the pride I now admire.
Hippolytus in love! What happy chance
Could bring me so to touch him . . .

ISMENE

                              You will hear.
He is coming to see you.

SCENE 2

Hippolytus, Aricia, Ismene

HIPPOLYTUS

                    Madam, before I go
I thought I should inform you how things stand.   485
My father is no more. I had misgivings
As to what made him stay so long away.
Only death, putting an end to his great deeds,
Could hide him from the world for so long.
The gods have yielded to a homicide Fate   490
The friend, the comrade, the successor of Hercules.
I think your hate will spare my father's virtues
And not resent these titles he has earned.
One hope alone mitigates my distress:
I can release you from a guardianship   495
Which was austere, and I revoke the laws
Which, to my mind, have been too rigorous.
Dispose of yourself, and your heart, as you will.
In this Troezene which has fallen to me
As once belonging to my mother's family,   500
And has at once recognized me as king,
I leave you free—and freer than myself.

ARICIA

Ah, do not carry your kindness to excess.
To be so generous to my low condition,

My lord, is more than you suppose, to bind me   505
Under the austere laws you release me from.

HIPPOLYTUS

Athens cannot decide on a successor;
They talk of you; name me and the queen's son.

ARICIA

Of me, my lord?

HIPPOLYTUS

              I know, to put it bluntly,
They have grand laws which seem to exclude me.   510
The Greeks object, my mother is a foreigner.
But, if my only rival were my brother,
Madam, I have a better claim than he
And I would make it good, law or no law.
What gives me pause has more justification.   515
I yield to you, or rather give you back
A sceptre which your ancestors received
From the great mortal who was the Earth's child.
Adoption passed it on to Aegeus.
Athens, to whom my father gave protection,   520
Joyfully recognized him as their king
And your unfortunate brothers were forgotten.
Now Athens calls you back within her walls,
Having suffered enough from this long quarrel
And seen enough of your family's blood   525
Soaking the very fields which gave it birth.
Troezene obeys me, and Phaedra's son
Will find a haven in the Cretan lands.
Attica is yours, and it is for you*
I go now to unite your friends and mine.   530

ARICIA

All this is so astonishing, so confusing,
I fear it may be nothing but a dream.
Am I awake? Is this to be believed?
What god, my lord, filled you with this intent?
Everywhere people praise you, and no wonder,   535
But the reality goes beyond any praise.
You are betraying yourself to favour me!
It would have been enough not to hate me,

To have been able to preserve your heart
So long from this hostility . . .

HIPPOLYTUS

                                        I, hate you?   540
Whatever has been said about my pride,
Do they suppose my mother was a monster?
What savage habits and what callous hate
Would not be gentler at the sight of you?
Could I resist the misleading charm . . .   545

ARICIA

What, my lord?

HIPPOLYTUS

                  I see I've gone too far.
Reason is giving way to violence,
But since I have begun to tell my thoughts,
Madam, I must go on; I must explain
The secret which my heart cannot conceal.   550
   You see before you an unfortunate prince,
A memorable example of rash pride.
I who, a vain rebel against love,
Have long despised the chains that bind her prisoners;
Who, contemplating other mortals' shipwrecks,   555
Always imagined I was safe on shore,
But now, subject to tempests like the rest,
I see myself swept far from myself.
I was audacious and imprudent; suddenly
The vaunting mind has become dependent.   560
For nearly six months, ashamed and desperate,
Trailing the arrow that is in my side,
I have struggled against you, against myself:
In your presence, I must get away;
In your absence, I see nothing but you.   565
The light of day, the shadows of the night
All conjure up the charms I would escape.
Hippolytus is yours, to do as you will with.
The only benefit I have from all this
Is looking for myself and finding no one.   570
My bow, my javelins, and chariot all mean nothing,
I have forgotten the art that Neptune taught me.

The forests now hear nothing but my sighs,
My horses graze and never hear my voice.
    Perhaps the story of so wild a love   575
Will make you blush to hear of your handiwork.
What a rough way to offer you my heart!
What a strange prisoner for so fine a bond!
But that should make the offering all the dearer.
Consider: love, for me, is a foreign language;   580
Do not reject the ill-expressed vows
Hippolytus would never have felt but for you.

SCENE 3

Hippolytus, Aricia, Theramenes, Ismene

THERAMENES
    My lord, the queen is coming, I came on ahead.
    She is looking for you.

HIPPOLYTUS

                            Me?

THERAMENES
                                    But what she wants
    I do not know; that is the message she sent.   585
    Phaedra must speak to you before you go.

HIPPOLYTUS
    Phaedra? What can I say? What's in her mind?

ARICIA
    My lord, you cannot say you will not listen.
    Although so certain of her enmity
    You must have some compassion on her tears.   590

HIPPOLYTUS
    Yet you are not staying. And I am leaving
    Without knowing whether I have offended you
    Or whether this heart of mine which is all yours . . .

ARICIA
    Go, prince, pursue your generous design.
    Let Attica submit herself to me.   595
    Everything that you offer, I accept.

But this great empire, glorious though it is,
Is not your best present, in my eyes.

SCENE 4

Hippolytus, Theramenes

HIPPOLYTUS

All ready, my friend? But here comes the queen.
Go, see that they give the signal, run, hurry back   600
And so release me from an awkward dialogue.

SCENE 5

Phaedra, Hippolytus, Oenone

PHAEDRA, to *Oenone*.

He is here. My blood rushes to my heart;
Seeing him, I forget what I have to say.

OENONE

Think of your son, whose only hope you are.

PHAEDRA

They say that you are leaving soon, my lord.   605
I come to weep with you for what you mourn.
I come to tell you my fears for my son.
My son has now no father; before long
He will be witness of my own death too.
He is a child and has a thousand enemies: 610
Only you can take charge of his defence.
I fear I may have made you deaf to his cries.
I know you have good reason to be angry
And tremble lest you should avenge on him
The wrongs done you by his hateful mother.   615

HIPPOLYTUS

Madam, I have no such unworthy feelings.

PHAEDRA

If you did hate me, I should not complain,
My lord; for you have seen me try to hurt you;
You cannot read what is in my heart.

I have tried hard to incur your hostility,   620
Not wanting you where I was living myself:
In public or in private I have declared
I wanted there to be oceans between us.
I even made it an absolute law
That no one should utter your name in my presence. 625
But if the offence is matched with the penalty,
If only hatred could attract your hatred,
Never was woman more to be pitied
And never any less deserved your enmity.

HIPPOLYTUS

A child's rights come first, with a jealous mother;   630
A son by another wife is rarely pardoned.
I know that, madam; continual suspicions
Are ordinary in a second marriage.
Another woman would have felt as you did;
Perhaps indeed I should have been treated worse.   635

PHAEDRA

Ah my lord, heaven, I swear here and now,
Excepted me from this general law!
I am consumed by very different trouble!

HIPPOLYTUS

Madam, this is no time to trouble you further.
It may be that your husband is still alive;   640
Heaven may, in pity, bring him back again.
Neptune is his protector and this god
Will not be deaf to my father's prayers.

PHAEDRA

No man can see the shores of Acheron twice,
My lord. Since Theseus has set eyes on them   645
It is vain to hope a god will send him back;
The hungry stream does not give up its prey.
What am I saying? He still breathes in you.
With you before my eyes, I see my husband.
Yes, see him, speak to him, my heart . . . I'm wandering,   650
My lord; my passion shows in spite of myself.

HIPPOLYTUS

Your love has this miraculous effect.

Dead though he is, Theseus appears before you;
Your love for him has set your mind on fire.

PHAEDRA

Yes, prince, I pine, I burn for Theseus. 655
I love him, not as in the underworld,
The fickle admirer of a thousand objects,
He travels to dishonour even the dead;
But as he was once, loyal and proud,
Even a little shy, charming and young 660
And drawing everybody's hearts to him,
As gods are said to be, as you are.
He had your bearing, eyes, your way of talking;
He even showed a noble diffidence
That time he came across our Cretan waves; 665
Minos' daughters well might love him then.
What were you doing then? Why did he gather
All the best men of Greece, and not Hippolytus?
Why were you then too young to be in that ship
Which set him down upon the shores of Crete? 670
The Minotaur would have died at your hands
In spite of all the turnings of his maze.
It would have been you my sister gave the thread to,
To find the way through these uncertainties.
But no: for I should have been there before her; 675
Love would have put the thought into my head.
I should have been the one to help you, prince,
And shown you all the turnings of the labyrinth;
What would I not have done for that charming head?
A thread would not have been enough for me: 680
I should have accompanied you in your danger,
Loving, I should have wanted to go first;
If Phaedra had been with you in the labyrinth
She would either have stayed with you or perished.

HIPPOLYTUS

Gods! What is it I hear? You forget, madam, 685
That Theseus is my father, and your husband!

PHAEDRA

What makes you think I have forgotten, prince?
Do you suppose I don't know who I am?

HIPPOLYTUS

    Madam, forgive me: with shame I admit it,
    I misinterpreted an innocent speech.   690
    I cannot stay here, having so disgraced myself
    And I am going . . .

PHAEDRA

                Do not be so cruel!
    You understood too well, and what I said
    Was quite enough to enlighten you.
    Well then, know Phaedra in all her fury.   695
    I am in love. Do not suppose that, loving you,
    I think myself innocent or approve myself;
    Nor that the poison which disturbs my reason
    Is fed by a compliance on my part.
    I am the victim of celestial vengeance   700
    And hate myself still more than you detest me.
    The gods will be my witnesses, these same gods
    Who lit that flame fatal to all my race;
    The very gods who have so cruelly gloried
    In the seduction of a weak mortal.   705
    Turn over the past now in your own mind:
    Not content to avoid you, I turned you out;
    I tried to appear odious and inhuman;
    The better to resist you, I sought your hatred.
    And what good did it do me, all this trouble?   710
    You hated me more, I did not love you less.
    Your spell was even stronger in your misfortunes,
    I pined, I shrivelled up, in flames, in tears.
    You have only to use your eyes to know it's true,
    If you could bear to look at me for a moment.   715
    What am I saying? This confession I've made,
    Do you suppose that it is voluntary?
    Trembling for a son I dared not betray,
    I came simply to ask you not to hate him.
    How feeble is a heart too full of love!   720
    I found that I could talk of no one but you!
    Take your revenge, punish my odious passion,
    Hero's son as you are, and what a hero!
    Rid the world of a monster you cannot bear.
    Theseus' widow dares to love Hippolytus!   725

The frightful monster must not get away.
Here is my heart. It is there your hand should strike.
Already I feel it though you have not struck.
Strike now: or if you think me not worth a blow,
If your hate grudges me so sweet a punishment,   730
Or my blood is too vile for you to shed,
If your arm falters, let me have your sword.
Now!

OENONE

      What are you doing, ma'am? Just heavens!
Someone is coming. Witnesses you would hate.
Come with me and avoid certain exposure.   735

SCENE 6

Hippolytus, Theramenes

THERAMENES

Is that Phaedra, in flight—no, dragged away?
You look like death, what is it, my dear lord?
I see you without your sword, speechless, white-faced!

HIPPOLYTUS

Theramenes, we must go. I am thunder-struck.
I have become a horror to myself.   740
Phaedra . . . But no, great gods. Complete oblivion
Must bury for ever so horrible a secret.

THERAMENES

If you wish to leave, we are ready to sail.
But, my lord, Athens has already decided;
The tribes have been consulted, and have spoken: 745
Your brother carried the day; Phaedra has won.

HIPPOLYTUS

Phaedra?

THERAMENES

      A herald with a proclamation
Has come from Athens, power is in her hands.
Her son is king, my lord.

HIPPOLYTUS

               You know her, gods.
Is it her virtue that you are rewarding?   750

THERAMENES

Meanwhile a rumour says the king's alive.
It is said that Theseus was seen in Epirus.
But I was there, my lord, I know too well . . .

HIPPOLYTUS

No matter; we must pick up every rumour.
We must follow this up and go to the source.   755
If there is nothing in it to deflect me,
We must go, and be the cost what it may,
Put the sceptre into hands fit to bear it.

ACT III

SCENE 1

Phaedra, Oenone

PHAEDRA

I want no honours, take them all away!
This is not the time ... Do you want me to be seen?   760
What hope can you offer my desolate mind?
Hide me rather: I have talked too much already.
My madness has dared to spill abroad;
I have said things which are not fit to be heard.
Heavens! How he listened to me! How unfeelingly   765
He took every occasion to miss my meaning,
All the time thinking only of escape.
And how he blushed, to shame me all the more!
Why did you turn me from my thoughts of death?
Alas! when his sword was pointed at my heart,   770
Did he grow pale for my sake? Did he snatch it?
It was enough that my hand had touched it;
That made it too horrible in his eyes
And he refused to soil his hands with it.

OENONE

Complaining will not help you in your trouble,   775
It merely fans the flames you should put out.
The race of Minos would be better served
By seeking nobler ways to find relief;
Turn on the fugitive in his ingratitude,
Reign, and assume direction of a State.   780

PHAEDRA

I, reign? I, turn law-giver to a State,
Who am too weak to reign over myself?
When I have lost control of my desires,
When I am choking under a load of shame,
When I am dying?

OENONE

              Escape!

PHAEDRA
                    I can't leave him!   785

OENONE
    You dared to banish him, yet won't avoid him!

PHAEDRA
    It is too late: he knows I am mad with love.
    The frontiers of restraint have been crossed;
    I have admitted my shame to my conqueror;
    In spite of myself, I have begun to hope.   790
    Was it not you recalled my failing strength
    And the last breath which hung upon my lips?
    You were the flatterer who revived me then;
    You made me see there was still time to love him.

OENONE
    What should I not have been capable of   795
    To save you from misfortune, innocent or not?
    But, if his scorn ever offended you,
    How can you now forget his arrogance?
    How cruel his eyes were when with obstinate rigour
    He left you more or less prostrate at his feet!   800
    How hateful he was in his savage pride!
    I wish that Phaedra had had my eyes then!

PHAEDRA
    Oenone, he may not always be so fierce.
    He was brought up in the woods and is rough like them.
    Hippolytus has been hardened by savage laws   805
    And this is the first time he has heard of love.
    Perhaps it was the surprise that made him silent
    And maybe our complaints are overdone.

OENONE
    Remember that his mother was a savage.

PHAEDRA
    A Scythian savage perhaps, but she loved.   810

OENONE
    He has a savage hate for the whole sex.

PHAEDRA
    So I shall not see some rival preferred.
    Anyhow, all your advice is too late now;

Do as my madness says, forget my reason.
Since his heart is insensible to love,   815
Let us attack him somewhere that hurts more.
The charm of being king is something to him.
Athens attracted him, he could not conceal it:
His ships were already pointed out to sea,
The sails were already flapping in the wind.   820
An ambitious young man! Go to him from me,
Oenone; dangle the crown before his eyes.
Let him put the sacred diadem on his head:
What an honour for me if I could set it there!
Let him have this authority, I can't keep it.   825
He will show my son how to take command;
Perhaps he will be a father to the boy:
I give him authority over son and mother.
Try every way you can to bring him round:
You will talk more persuasively than I should.   830
Argue, weep, moan, pity the dying Phaedra;
Entreat him shamelessly and, mind, no blushes!
I shall back all you say; I've no hope but you.
Go: when you come back I will do what I will.

SCENE 2

PHAEDRA, *alone.*

O you who see to what shame I have sunk,   835
Implacable Venus! am I low enough?
You cannot push your cruelty any further.
Your triumph is complete: every dart went home.
Cruel goddess, if you look for fresh glory,
Attack an enemy who will rebel against you.   840
Hippolytus is running away now;
Braving your anger, he has ignored your altars
And he has always treated your name with scorn.
Goddess, take your revenge: your cause is mine.
Make him be in love ... You're back already,   845
Oenone? So he hates me and won't listen?

SCENE 3

Phaedra, Oenone

OENONE

You must give up the futile thought of love,
Ma'am. Summon all your old virtue:
You will soon see the king we thought dead;
Theseus has come, Theseus is with us here.   850
The mob run to fling themselves upon him.
I was on the way, as you ordered, to Hippolytus,
When a thousand voices shouted to high heaven . . .

PHAEDRA

My husband lives, Oenone, that is enough.
I have confessed a love which insults him;   855
He is alive: I want to hear no more.

OENONE

What?

PHAEDRA

    I told you, but you would not listen:
I was remorseful, your tears won me over.
Had I died this morning, I'd have been worth tears;
I followed your advice: I die dishonoured.   860

OENONE

You die?

PHAEDRA

    Just heavens! What have I done today?
My husband's coming and his son with him.
I shall see the witness of my adulterous passion
Watching my face as I receive his father,
My heart heavy with sighs he will not listen to,   865
My eye moist with tears his ingratitude scorned.
Do you think that, careful of Theseus's honour,
He will conceal from him what troubles me?
Let treason touch his father and his king?
Could he contain the horror that he feels?   870
It would be useless: I know my perfidy,
Oenone, I am not a brazen woman

Who enjoys quiet in the midst of crime
And puts on a good face whatever happens.
I know my madness, I remember everything.   875
Already it seems that these walls, these arches,
Will start to speak and, ready to accuse me,
Are waiting only till my husband comes.
Let me die and death save me from these horrors.
Is it so terrible to cease to live?   880
Death cannot frighten those who are unhappy.
All I fear is the name I leave behind me.
What worse thing could my poor children inherit?
They must have courage, coming of Jupiter's blood,
But, proud though they may justly be of that,   885
A mother's crime is a heavy load to bear.
I tremble lest one day someone, too truly,
Should reproach them because of their mother's guilt.
I tremble lest, under the weight of this foul load,
Neither of them dares raise his downcast eyes.   890

OENONE

No question, it is so; I pity them both;
You are right, certainly, to fear for them.
But why must you expose them to these insults?
Why must you turn witness against yourself?
Will it not then be said that Phaedra, guilty,   895
Could not endure her injured husband's eyes?
Hippolytus will find it excellent
That you should die and so confirm his story.
And how shall I answer your accuser?
With him there I shall never hold my own.   900
I shall see him delighted with his triumph,
Telling your shame to anyone who will listen.
Ah, rather let me be struck by lightning!
Tell me the truth, how does the prince look now?

PHAEDRA

I see him now as a frightful monster.   905

OENONE

Then why allow him absolute victory?
You are afraid of him: but dare instead
To accuse him before he accuses you.

Who will doubt you then? Everything is against him:
The sword he happily left in your hands,   910
Your present trouble and your past distress
And your complaints which should have warned him,
The fact that it was you asked for his exile.

PHAEDRA

Am I then to destroy an innocent man?

OENONE

All I require of you is your silence.   915
I tremble as you do, I feel some remorse.
I would rather insult a thousand of the dead.
But since, without this remedy, I lose you,
Your life for me comes before everything:
I'll do the talking. Theseus, when I've roused him,   920
Will do no more than exile his dear son:
A father, ma'am, punishes like a father
And a light punishment satisfies his anger.
But suppose innocent blood had to be shed,
What does a threat to your honour not demand?   925
It is too precious to be put in question.
Whatever it dictates, that you must do.
Ma'am, to secure that your honour is safe,
All must be sacrificed, and even virtue.
Someone is coming, I see Theseus.   930

PHAEDRA

I see Hippolytus, and in his eyes,
An insolent intention to destroy me.
Do what you will, I let you have your way.
In this confusion I cannot help myself.

SCENE 4

Theseus, Hippolytus, Phaedra, Oenone, Theramenes

THESEUS

Destiny, madam, is no longer hostile,   935
It throws me into your arms . . .

PHAEDRA

                                        Stop, Theseus:

Do not profane a moment of delight.
I am no longer worthy of such a welcome;
Your honour is at stake. While you were absent
The envy of fortune has not spared your wife.   940
I am not fit to please you or come near you;
Henceforth I can think only of concealment.

SCENE 5

Theseus, Hippolytus, Theramenes

THESEUS
What is behind this strange reception, son?

HIPPOLYTUS
Phaedra alone can explain this mystery.
If my intensest wishes count for anything,   945
My lord, permit me not to see her again;
Allow Hippolytus, trembling, to disappear
For ever from wherever your wife lives.

THESEUS
You are leaving me?

HIPPOLYTUS
                    It was not I who sought her;
It was you yourself who brought her to these shores.   950
You deigned, my lord, to entrust to Troezene,
When you went away, Aricia and the queen.
You even charged me to look after them.
But now there is no further need for that.
Enough of my idle youth has passed   955
Chasing after easy prey in the forests:
Can I now give up such recreations
And blood my javelin with nobler game?
Before you were as old as I am now,
More than one tyrant, more than one wild monster,   960
Had felt what strength there was in your arm;
Already you had successfully pursued
Wild beasts and robbers, and cleared the coast roads;
The traveller was free to go unhindered;
Hercules paused when he heard the story,   965

Confident that he could leave such tasks to you.
And I, the unknown son of such a father,
Am myself still outstripped by my mother.
Allow my courage to find occupation.
Allow me, if any monster has escaped you,   970
To take its spoils and lay them at your feet,
Or else to leave a lasting memory
Of days well spent and ended fittingly
To prove for all time that I was your son.

THESEUS

What is this? What horrible thing has happened   975
To make my family run from my sight?
If I am so feared and so unwanted,
Why, heavens, did you release me from my prison?
I had no friends but one: his imprudent passion
Fixed on the wife of the tyrant of Epirus;   980
Reluctantly, I helped him in his schemes;
But fate was against us and made us both blind.
The tyrant took me, defenceless, without arms.
I saw Pirithoüs, with tears I saw him
Delivered by the tyrant to the cruel monsters   985
He was accustomed to feed on human blood.
Me he shut up inside a dark cavern
Deep in the earth, by the kingdom of the dead.
It was six months before the gods looked at me:
I managed to deceive the eyes that guarded me   990
And my perfidious enemy had his deserts
For he himself became food for his monsters.
And then, when with delight I came back
To everything I hold most dear on earth,
When my soul, once again its own master,   995
Comes here to take its fill of these dear sights,
The only welcome I find is a shudder;
They fly from me, they refuse my embraces;
And I, feeling the terror I inspire,
Would gladly be back in my old prison.   1000
Speak. Phaedra says it is a question of honour:
Who has betrayed me? Why am I not avenged?
Has Greece, which my arm has often served,
Been giving sanctuary to the criminal?

You do not answer. My son, my own son,   1005
Has after all sided with my enemies?
Let us go in: doubt is intolerable.
Let me know what the crime was and who did it:
Phaedra must say what this great trouble is.

SCENE 6

Hippolytus, Theramenes

HIPPOLYTUS

What did she mean by saying what she did?   1010
Can Phaedra, in her terrifying madness,
Intend to accuse herself, and court destruction?
Gods! What will the king say? What deadly poison
Love has spilt everywhere on this family!
As for me, full of a passion he must hate,   1015
He finds me as I was before he left.
The darkest of presentiments close upon me.
Yet surely innocence has nothing to fear.
Come, let us once more try with what skill
I can revive my father's tenderness   1020
And tell him of a love he may impede
But which even his authority cannot shake.

ACT IV

SCENE 1

Theseus, Oenone

THESEUS

What are you telling me? A reckless traitor
Was ready to outrage his father's honour?
Fate! with what rigour you pursue me still! 1025
Where am I going? Where indeed am I?
So much for tenderness, so much for kindness!
All the return I get is to be made
The victim of his filthy enterprise.
To reach the object of his lust the rascal 1030
Thought nothing of employing violence.
I recognized the sword he meant to use,
The sword I gave him for a better purpose.
The ties of blood were no restraint to him!
And Phaedra did not want to have him punished! 1035
Her silence would have saved the criminal!

OENONE

Phaedra thought more of saving you, my lord.
So ashamed was she of her furious lover
And of the passion blazing in his eyes,
Phaedra wanted to die, her murderous hand 1040
Was turned against her own innocent life.
I saw her raise her arm, I rescued her;
I it was who preserved her for your love
And, pitying her fears and your anxiety,
I have, I could not help it, told you everything. 1045

THESEUS

So treacherous! no wonder he grew pale:
I saw him shudder, frightened, when he greeted me.
I was astounded that he showed no pleasure;
His coldness when we met froze my affection.
But had this guilty love that devours him 1050
Already shown itself when they were in Athens?

OENONE

My lord, recall how the queen complained:
It was this criminal love caused all her hatred.

THESEUS

Then it began again in Troezene?

OENONE

I have told you what happened here, my lord.   1055
The queen must not be left, in her agony;
Permit me to leave you now and go to her.

SCENE 2

Theseus, Hippolytus

THESEUS

Ah, here he is. Great gods, he looks fine,
What eyes but would have been deceived as mine were?
Why must the face of an adulterer   1060
Shine with the look of a religious virtue?
And should it not be possible to find
Some trace of a perfidious human heart?

HIPPOLYTUS

May I enquire, my lord, what deadly cloud
It is that so troubles your august looks?   1065
Do you not dare to trust me with this secret?

THESEUS

Traitor, you dare show yourself before me?
Monster, you should have been struck by lightning!
I thought I had cleared the earth of such brigands,
But even after an appalling passion   1070
Which did not pause even at your father's bed,
You dare to come here, enemy that you are?
You appear in a place full of your infamy
Instead of looking for some unknown place
In some country where no one has heard of me?   1075
Make your escape, traitor. Do not brave my hatred
And tempt an anger I can barely restrain:
It is enough opprobrium for me
That I gave life to a son so criminal,
Without soiling the glory of my labours   1080

By adding to them the infamy of your death.
Get out; and unless you want instant punishment
By this hand which has punished so many reprobates,
Take care the light of heaven shall never see you
Rashly set foot in this country again.   1085
Get out, I say; be quick, cleanse my domains
Of your foul presence and do not return.

   And you, Neptune, you, if once my courage*
Cleared your shores of infamous assassins,
Remember that, as my reward, you promised   1090
To grant me the first boon that I would ask.
In all the time I was suffering in prison
I did not once invoke your immortal power:
I set too high a value on your help,
And kept you for a greater occasion than that.   1095
Now I invoke you. Avenge an unhappy father;
I give this traitor over to all your anger;
Choke in his blood his insolent desires:
Theseus will see your fury as a kindness.

HIPPOLYTUS
Phaedra accuses me of a criminal love!   1100
The excess of horror leaves my spirit dumb;
So many blows overwhelming me at once
Make me silent, and my voice chokes me.

THESEUS
Traitor, you hoped that Phaedra would keep quiet
And weakly hide your brutal insolence: 1105
In that case you should not have left your sword
Which in her hands is evidence against you:
Or rather you should, to complete your perfidy,
Have stopped her mouth and taken her life at once.

HIPPOLYTUS
Justly outraged at so black a lie,   1110
I should attempt to make the truth speak here,
My lord; but it touches you too nearly,
I suppress the secret, and you should approve
This respect for you which makes me keep my mouth shut.
Do not yourself multiply your troubles: 1115
Consider my life, consider who I am.

There are always crimes of some sort before there are great ones.
Anyone who has once crossed the boundaries
Of right and wrong may stop at no impiety:
Like virtue, crime itself has some degrees,   1120
And never has timid innocence been seen
To pass in a moment to extreme licence.
A single day does not turn a virtuous mortal
To murder, perfidy, and cowardly incest.
Brought up by a chaste, courageous mother,   1125
I have not belied the origin of her blood.
Pittheus, thought the wisest of humanity,
Deigned to instruct me when I was out of her hands.
I do not wish to claim that I am perfect;
But, if I have any virtues at all,   1130
My lord, I think I can claim to have demonstrated
Hatred of the enormities I am accused of.
Hippolytus is known over all Greece
For carrying virtue to the point of boorishness
And my displeasure is inflexible.   1135
Deep in my heart all is pure as day.
If it is said that Hippolytus profaned . . .

THESEUS

Yes, and it is this same pride that condemns you,
Which is the odious cause of your chilliness:
Phaedra so charmed your lascivious eyes,   1140
You were indifferent to all other objects
And scorned the notion of an innocent love.

HIPPOLYTUS

No, father, I cannot hide from you that my heart
Was far from showing scorn for a chaste passion.
At your feet I will confess my true offence.   1145
I am in love, a love you have forbidden.
Aricia holds me fast under her sway.
The daughter of Pallas has subdued your son.
I worship her; in spite of your commands
I sigh, I burn, my heart and soul are hers.   1150

THESEUS

You love her? No you don't, it is too plain
You say you do to justify yourself.

HIPPOLYTUS
> My lord, for six months I have avoided her
> Because I love her, I came here to confess it.
> Ah, nothing can remove your misconception!   1155
> What can I swear by that will reassure you?
> May earth and heaven, may the whole creation ...

THESEUS
> Evil men always have recourse to perjury.
> Stop, this is not the time for that sort of talk,
> If your pretence can think of nothing else.   1160

HIPPOLYTUS
> You think it a pretence and think me devious:
> But Phaedra, at the bottom of her heart,
> Knows better and will do me that justice.

THESEUS
> Your impudence is driving me to anger!

HIPPOLYTUS
> How long must I be exiled, in what place?   1165

THESEUS
> If you were out beyond the Pillars of Hercules,
> I should consider you too close a neighbour!

HIPPOLYTUS
> Charged with the crime that you suspect me of,
> No friend will pity me, if you abandon me.

THESEUS
> Go and find friends who esteem what is worst,   1170
> Who honour adultery and applaud incest;
> Traitors, without honour, graceless, lawless,
> Fit to protect a renegade like you.

HIPPOLYTUS
> You still talk of incest and adultery:
> I say nothing. But Phaedra had a mother,   1175
> Phaedra is of a race, as you well know,
> My lord, more full of horrors than my own.*

THESEUS
> What! have you lost all sense of decency?
> For the last time I say, get out of my sight!

Out, traitor! do not wait for an outraged father   1180

To send you from this place as you deserve.

SCENE 3

THESEUS, *alone.*

Outcast, you will infallibly be lost!
Neptune has sworn by all that the gods fear;
He has given his word, he will accomplish it.
You cannot escape from an avenging god.   1185
I loved you and I feel, despite your offence,
Profoundly troubled by your certain fate.
But you have forced me to this condemnation:
Was ever any father so dishonoured?
Just gods, who see the pains that overwhelm me,   1190
Can I have given life to such a child?

SCENE 4

Phaedra, Theseus

PHAEDRA

My lord, I come to you truly in terror.
I could not help but hear the threats you made:
I am afraid now of what has followed.
If there is still time, spare your family,   1195
Think of your noble blood, I dare entreat you;
Spare me the horror of hearing it cry out;
Let me not feel the everlasting pain
Of having provoked a father's hand to shed it.

THESEUS

No, madam, my hand is clean of my own blood;   1200
And yet the graceless boy has not escaped me:
An immortal hand is charged with his destruction;
Neptune is in my debt, you will be avenged.

PHAEDRA

Neptune is in your debt! What, have you prayed ...

THESEUS

Are you afraid my prayers will not be heard?   1205

Join in them rather, they are justified:
Tell me the full horror of his crimes;
Incite me, I have been perhaps too gentle.
Some of his crimes you still do not know of:
His fury has gone so far as to insult you.   1210
Your lips, he says, are nothing but deceit.
He asserts that he is pledged to Aricia,
That he loves her.

PHAEDRA

               My lord?

THESEUS

                          That is what he said,
But I know better and I told him so.
Let us hope Neptune will do justice quickly: 1215
I am going now to plead before his altars
For the accomplishment of what he has sworn.

SCENE 5

PHAEDRA, *alone.*

He has gone. And what is this news I hear?
What smouldering flames begin to revive?
I am struck by lightning, heavens, it is death!   1220
I was about to go to my son's aid;
Wrenching myself from Oenone, who was terrified,
I was giving way to the remorse I felt.
Who knows how far repentance would have carried me?
Perhaps I should have dared to accuse myself.   1225
Perhaps if I had not been interrupted
The truth in all its horror would have come out.
Hippolytus can feel love, but not for me!
Pledged to Aricia! to Aricia!
Ah, gods! When he refused to listen to me,   1230
Put on so proud a look, so stern a face,
I thought his heart, for ever closed to love,
Was armed against all members of my sex:
Another woman has broken his pride;
His cruel eyes have softened for someone else,   1235
Perhaps his heart is after all easily touched:

I am the only person he cannot stand.
And I undertook to defend him!

SCENE 6

Phaedra, Oenone

PHAEDRA

Oenone, do you know what I've found out?

OENONE

No; but I come here trembling, to tell the truth: 1240
I went white to think why you had gone;
I feared your fury was turned against yourself.

PHAEDRA

Oenone, who would have thought it possible?
I have a rival.

OENONE

             What?

PHAEDRA

             No doubt about it,
Hippolytus is in love; he, so hostile,   1245
The wild man whom nobody could tame,
Who shied away at respect, would hear no complaints
—Submissive, tractable, recognizes his conqueror:
Aricia has found the way to his heart.

OENONE

Aricia?

PHAEDRA

            I have never suffered like this!   1250
For what new torment have I preserved myself!
All I have been through, all my fears, my transports,
The fury of love, the horror of remorse,
The insupportable insult of refusal,
All was nothing to what I now endure.   1255
They love one another! How did they deceive me?
How have they managed to meet? Since when? And where?
You knew it: why did you let me hope at all?
Could you not have told me of their furtive passion?

Have they often been seen talking together?   1260
Used they to go and hide themselves in the woods?
Ah, they could quite easily see one another:
The heavens approved, their sighs were innocent;
They could love as they would without remorse;
Every day dawned bright and clear for them!   1265
And I, rejected by all creation,
Hid myself from the day, fled from the light;
Death is the only god I dared implore.
The only hope I had was to expire.
Feeding myself with gall, watered by tears,   1270
Too closely watched even in misfortune,
I dared not even drown myself with weeping,
Trembling when I enjoyed this fatal pleasure,
But, showing a calm face amidst all alarms,
I often had to do without even tears.   1275

OENONE

What good will their love ever do them?
They will never meet again.

PHAEDRA

                                   They will still be in love!
Even as I speak—there is death in the thought—
They challenge the fury of a demented queen!
In spite of the very exile which will divide them   1280
They are swearing they will never leave one another!
No, I cannot bear an insulting happiness.
Pity my jealousy and rage, Oenone.
Aricia must be destroyed. My husband's anger
Must once more fasten on that odious race.   1285
There must be no limit to the punishment:
The sister's crime is worse than all her brothers'.
Jealous as I am I will implore him to act.
     What am I doing? I am out of my mind!
I, jealous! And it is Theseus I implore!   1290
My husband is alive and I still on fire!
For whom? And whose heart is it I am claiming?
Every word makes my hair stand on end!
My crimes from now on have reached the top:
I am nothing now but incest and imposture,   1295

My homicide hands, so anxious for revenge,
Are burning to be dipped in innocent blood.
I am lost! And I live! I can bear the eye
Of this sacred Sun from which I am descended!
My ancestor is the father of all the gods;   1300
The heavens, the universe is full of my ancestors:
Where can I hide? Let it be in infernal night.
What do I say? My father holds the urn there;*
Fate, so they say, has put it in his hands.
Minos in hell is judge of all pale mortals.   1305
Ah! how his shade will tremble in alarm
When he sees his daughter, there before his eyes,
Forced to confess to such enormities,
To crimes perhaps that hell has never known!
What will you say, father, when you see this?   1310
The terrible urn will fall from your hands;
I think I see you, looking for a new punishment,
The executioner of your own flesh and blood.
Pardon, father. A cruel god breaks your family;
You see his vengeance in your daughter's madness.   1315
Alas! my broken heart has never plucked
The fruit of the crime, though the shame follows me:
Pursued by misfortune to my last sigh,
I yield a pitiful life which ends in torment.

OENONE

But, ma'am, there is no need for such terror.   1320
Consider, is your error not excusable?
You are in love. Destiny is invincible:
You were the victim of a fatal charm.
Is that such a prodigy among us?
Are you the only one love has triumphed over?   1325
The weakness is a common one enough.
You are only mortal, it is a mortal's lot.
What you complain of is not a new burden:
Even the gods inhabiting Olympus,
Who rage so terrifyingly at crimes,   1330
Have sometimes flared up in illicit loves.

PHAEDRA

What do I hear? You dare give me such counsels?

So you would poison me right to the end,
Woman of ill omen! You have destroyed me.
I fled from the light and you called me back,   1335
You entreated me, and I forgot my duty;
I shrank from Hippolytus, you would have none of it.
What do you want to do? When you accused him,
Why did you impiously speak ill of him?
The consequence is, perhaps, that he will die,   1340
His father's sacrilegious prayer perhaps answered.
I will listen to you no more. Go, monster,
Go now and leave me to my disastrous fate.
May a just heaven pay you as you deserve!
And may your punishment for ever terrify   1345
All who, like you, by cowardly subtleties,
Play to the weakness of unfortunate princes,
Encourage them in what they are disposed to,
And dare to make the way to crime easy:
Detestable flatterers, the most deadly gift   1350
The anger of the heavens can make to kings.

OENONE, *alone.*

Ah, gods, to serve her I have done all, lost all;
And now have my reward. I have deserved it.

ACT V

SCENE 1

Hippolytus, Aricia

ARICIA

    What! In this peril you can still be silent?
    You leave your father in his ignorance,   1355
    Although he loves you? O, you are cruel;
    If all my tears are powerless to move you
    And you consent never to see me again,
    Go, separate yourself from sad Aricia;
    But at least, as you go, save your own life,   1360
    Defend your honour from reproach and shame
    And force your father to call back his prayers:
    There is still time. Why must you recklessly
    Leave the field free to Phaedra's accusations?
    Explain to Theseus.

HIPPOLYTUS

               Where have I failed?   1365
    Should I have shown him that his bed was foul?
    Should I have told him so plain a story
    As would bring shame to any father's face?
    No one but you has this odious secret.
    My heart is known only to you and the gods.   1370
    I could not hide from you—judge whether I love you—
    All that I would have hidden from myself;
    But bear in mind under what seal of silence.
    Forget if you can what I told you, madam.
    And may you never open your pure mouth   1375
    To tell so horrible a misadventure;
    Let us trust to the justice of the gods:
    It is impossible they should not clear me;
    Sooner or later Phaedra will be punished
    And must incur a proper ignominy.   1380
    In nothing else do I demand obedience;
    As for the rest, my anger has its head:
    You are released from the slavery you are in;

Show your courage, follow me, stay with me;
Tear yourself from this deadly, profaned place   1385
Where virtue draws no breath that is not poisoned;
Now is the moment, while there is confusion
Because of my disgrace, for you to go.
I can make sure that you will get away:
It is still my men who have charge of you;   1390
Our quarrel will not lack powerful defenders;
Argos holds out its arms and Sparta calls us.
They are friends to us both and they will listen;
Phaedra must not profit from our misfortunes
To drive us both from the paternal throne,   1395
Or give her son what is despoiled from us.
This is our chance, let us seize it with both hands.
What is this fear which makes you hesitate?
It is your interest only which inspires me.
When I am full of fire, why are you ice?   1400
Are you afraid to follow a banished man?

ARICIA

Ah my lord, I should love such an exile!
With what delight, if our lots were united,
I should live cut off from all the rest of the world!
But, since we are not joined in that sweet union,   1405
How can I honourably steal away with you?
I know that without wrong to my honour
I can escape from your father's hands:
It would not be running away from my parents,
And flight is permissible for a prisoner.   1410
But my lord, you love me; my reputation . . .

HIPPOLYTUS

No, no, I care too much for your good name.
What brings me here is a more civil plan:
Escape your enemies and follow your husband.
Our troubles leave us free, and heaven approves   1415
That we should give ourselves to one another.
Marriage need not be celebrated with pomp.
    At the gates of Troezene, among the tombs
Where former princes of my race lie buried,
Is a sacred temple, proof against perjury.   1420

No mortal dares swear falsely in that place:
False oaths receive immediate punishment;
The fear of an inevitable death
Makes the place one where lies cannot live.
There we will go, if you give your consent,   1425
And there we will confirm our solemn vows.
The god who is worshipped there shall be our witness.
We will both pray that he will be our father.
I will swear by the holiest of the gods.
The chaste Diana and the august Juno,   1430
And all the gods who witness my tenderness
Will guarantee my holy promises.

ARICIA

The king is coming. Prince, you must go at once.
To conceal my departure, I will stay
One moment only. Leave some faithful guide   1435
Who will conduct my timid steps towards you.

SCENE 2

Theseus, Aricia, Ismene

THESEUS

Gods, lighten my darkness, and reveal
The truth my eyes are seeking here below!

ARICIA

Ismene dear, have everything ready.

SCENE 3

Theseus, Aricia

THESEUS

You colour and you seem to be struck dumb,   1440
Madam! What was Hippolytus doing here?

ARICIA

My lord, he came to take his last farewells.

THESEUS

Your eyes have tamed him, stubborn as he is,

And his first sighs are your handiwork.

ARICIA

My lord, I cannot deny what is true: 1445
He does not have his father's hatred of me;
He was not treating me as a criminal.

THESEUS

I understand: he swore eternal love.
Have no confidence in this wayward heart;
He used to swear just the same to others.   1450

ARICIA

He, my lord?

THESEUS

                    You should have had more hold on him.
How could you share this horrible love of his?

ARICIA

And how can you bear to speak so horribly,
And set a blight upon a noble life?
Have you so little knowledge of his heart?   1455
And can you not tell crime from innocence?
Must you alone see an odious cloud
Steal over his virtue, which shines for all other eyes?
Ah, it is teaching evil tongues to wag.
Stop now. Repent of your homicide prayers: 1460
There is danger, my lord, that the rigorous gods
May hate you enough to grant what you pray for:
Often in anger heaven accepts our victims;
Its gifts are often the penalty of our crimes.

THESEUS

No, you cannot cover up his foul act.   1465
Your love blinds you, graceless as he is.
But I have witnesses who are above suspicion:
I have seen real tears flowing, and I know.

ARICIA

Take care, my lord. Your invincible hands
Have freed men from innumerable monsters: 1470
But not all are destroyed, you have left alive
One . . . But your son, my lord, has sealed my lips.
I well know the respect in which he holds you,

And should offend against it if I spoke.
I imitate his discretion, I will leave you   1475
Before I am obliged to break my silence.

SCENE 4

THESEUS, *alone.*

What does she really think, what does it mean,
To start and stop and end by saying nothing?
Are they trying to throw dust in my eyes?
Are they in league to put me to the torture?   1480
Yet I, in spite of my severity,
Hear a cry at the bottom of my heart.
A secret pity has surprised me there.
I must again interrogate Oenone:
I must have further light upon this crime.   1485
Guards, tell Oenone to come here, alone.

SCENE 5

Theseus, Panope

PANOPE

I do not know what the queen is planning,
My lord, but fear the worst. She is agitated,
And I have never seen her so despairing;
There is a deathly pallor on her face.   1490
Already Oenone, dismissed in disgrace,
Has thrown herself into the depths of the sea.
Nobody knows why she has so acted;
And now she has gone from us we shall never know.

THESEUS

What do I hear?

PANOPE

             The queen is no calmer   1495
After this death, her trouble seems to grow.
Sometimes, as if to ease her secret griefs,

She hugs her children, bathing them in tears,
Then suddenly, there is an end to mother-love,
She pushes them away, it seems in horror.   1500
She paces here and there irresolutely;
Her eye is wild, she does not recognize us.
Three times she has written, and then changed her mind,
And three times torn up the letter she began.
Agree to see her, my lord, agree to help her.   1505

THESEUS

Oenone dead, and Phaedra wants to die?
Call back my son, let him defend himself;
Let him speak to me, I am ready to hear him.
Make no haste with the fatal boon you promised,
Neptune: better that you should never grant it.   1510
Perhaps I have given credit to doubtful witnesses;
Perhaps I raised my cruel hands to you too soon.
Ah, what despair, if my prayer is answered!

SCENE 6

Theseus, Theramenes

THESEUS

Theramenes, is that you? Where is my son?
I trusted you with him from his first days.   1515
But why these tears? Why are you shedding tears?
What is he doing now?

THERAMENES

                              It is too late
For tenderness. Hippolytus is dead.

THESEUS

Gods!

THERAMENES

            I have seen the best of mortals perish,
I dare, my lord, say, the most innocent.   1520

THESEUS

My son is gone? So, when I would embrace him,

The impatient gods have expedited his death?
What blow has taken him from me? What thunderbolt?

THERAMENES

We were just out of the gates of Troezene.
He was in his chariot; his troubled guards   1525
Copied his silence and all gathered round him.
Lost in thought, he took the Mycenae road;
His hands held the reins as slack as may be.
His proud stallions, which at other times
Were so eager to answer to his voice,   1530
Looked crestfallen now and bowed their heads,
Seeming to act out his sad reflections.
A terrible cry, coming from below the waves,
At this moment shattered the peaceful air;
And from the bowels of the earth a fearsome voice   1535
Replied with a groan to the appalling cry.
Our blood froze to the bottom of our hearts;
The stallions listened, their manes stood on end.
Meanwhile, upon the surface of the sea,
There rose a boiling mass, a liquid mountain;   1540
The wave came near; it broke, and spewed up
Before our eyes, from the foam, a furious monster.
Its broad head was armed with threatening horns;
Its whole body was covered with yellowy scales;
An untameable bull, an impetuous dragon,   1545
Its back was rippling into tortuous folds;
Its prolonged bellowings made the shore tremble.
The heavens saw this wild monster with horror,
The earth was moved, the air was infected;
The wave that brought it drew back fearfully.   1550
Everything fled, courage had become useless
And all sought refuge in the nearby temple.
Hippolytus alone, a hero's son,
Pulled up his stallions, seized his javelins,
Faced the monster and, with a well-aimed throw,   1555
Made a great wound in the monster's side.
At this the beast, bounding with rage and pain,
Fell roaring at the horses' feet, rolled over
And turned his flaming jaws in their direction;
They were covered with fire, with blood and with smoke.   1560

They took fright and bolted, neither rein nor voice
Could hold them any more. Their master, powerless,
Blazed up in useless effort to restrain them.
They made the bits red with a foam of blood.
Some say they saw, as the animals bolted,   1565
A god pressing his spurs in their dusty flanks.
Fear sent them hurtling across the rocks;
The axle screamed and broke; Hippolytus
Saw his chariot smashed into flying pieces;
He fell and was entangled in the reins.   1570
Excuse my grief: the sight remains with me
And will for ever bring tears to my eyes.
I saw, my lord, I saw your son helpless,
Dragged by the horses his own hands had fed.
He tried to speak to them, his voice scared them;   1575
They raced on. Soon he was one great wound.
The plain echoed with our cries of grief.
At last their impetuous movement slackened:
They stopped not far from those ancient tombs
Where kings, his ancestors, are silent relics.   1580
I ran up breathlessly, his guards followed:
The fresh tracks of his blood guided us;
The rocks were dyed with it; the ghastly brambles
Were marked by handfuls of his bloodied hair.
I reached him, spoke his name: he gave me his hand,   1585
Opened a dying eye and closed it suddenly.
'The heavens', he said, 'have taken an innocent life.
Take care of poor Aricia after my death.
Dear friend, if my father, one day undeceived,
Has pity for a son falsely accused,   1590
Tell him that to appease my blood and shade,
He needs only to treat his captive gently;
May he give her ...' With these words the hero
Left in my arms only a mangled body,
The sad effect of the gods' triumphant anger;   1595
Even his father would not recognize him.

THESEUS

My son! and I myself destroyed my hope!
Inexorable gods who too well served me!
What is my life now but mortal regret?

THERAMENES

> And then, timidly, Aricia arrived,   1600
> Seeking to avoid your anger, my lord,
> Before the gods to take him as a husband.
> She drew near. She saw the grass blood-red;
> She saw (what a sight for a lover's eyes!)
> Hippolytus stretched out shapeless and colourless.   1605
> At first she could not credit her unhappiness;
> No longer recognizing her adored hero,
> She saw Hippolytus and still asked for him.
> But, too sure at the last that this was he,
> In a sad glance she accused the gods   1610
> And, cold, moaning, almost inanimate,
> She fell in a faint at her lover's feet.
> Ismene was with her; Ismene, all tears,
> Brought her back to life, or rather, to grief.
> As for me, I have come, hating the light,   1615
> To tell you the last wish of a hero,
> And to acquit myself of the last duty
> Which my lord, as he died, he laid upon me.
> But I see here his mortal enemy.

SCENE 7

Theseus, Phaedra, Theramenes, Panope, Guards

THESEUS

> Well, so you triumph and my son is dead.   1620
> Ah, what must I not fear? A cruel suspicion,
> Excusing him in my heart, justly alarms me.
> But, madam, he is dead, accept your victim;
> Enjoy his loss, whether unjust or not:
> I will still let my eyes be deceived   1625
> And think him criminal, since you accuse him.
> His death leaves me enough room for tears
> Without my seeking odious explanations
> Which cannot give him back to my true grief
> And would perhaps only increase my pain.   1630
> Allow me, far from you, far from this shore,
> To get away from his mangled image.

In chaos, persecuted by memory,
I wish for nothing but my banishment.
Everything rises against my injustice;   1635
The greatness of my name adds to my torture:
If I were less known I could hide better.
I hate even the attentions of the gods;
I go where I may weep their murderous favours
Without wearying them more with useless prayers.   1640
Whatever they might do for me, no gift
Of theirs could ever pay for what they have taken.

PHAEDRA

No, Theseus, I must break an unjust silence;
Your son must have his innocence back again:
He was not guilty.

THESEUS

              Ah! Ill-fortuned father!   1645
And it was trusting you made me condemn him!
Cruel woman! And you make excuses . . .

PHAEDRA

Moments are precious, listen to me, Theseus:
It is I who, on this chaste, respectful son
Dared set a blasphemous, incestuous eye.   1650
The heavens lit in my breast a deadly flame;
The horrible Oenone did the rest.
She feared that Hippolytus, told of my mad love,
Might make it public, for he hated it.
Disloyally, and exploiting my weakness,   1655
She was quick to seek you out and accuse him.
She has punished herself. Escaping from my anger,
She drowned herself, it was too gentle an end.
The sword would have finished me already,
But I let the suspicion fall on virtue: 1660
I wanted to tell you all my remorse
And go down to the dead a slower way.
I have taken, I have set in my burning veins
A poison which Medea brought to Athens.
Already it is working in my heart   1665
And on my heart it casts an unknown chill;
Already I can see only mistily

The heavens and the husband I outraged;
And death, stealing the light from my eyes,
Restores the purity of the day they sullied.   1670

PANOPE
    She is going, my lord.

THESEUS
                    Well, let her go!
If only this foul action could go with her!
Come, it is too clear where my error lay,
Let us shed tears to mix with my son's blood.
All that remains of this unfortunate   1675
I will take up in a father's arms
And expiate my own detested prayer.
Give him the honours he too well deserved;
And, that we may the more appease his spirit,
From this day forth, despite her family's treason,   1680
Let her he loved be welcomed as my daughter.

ATHALIAH

tragedy drawn
from Holy Scripture

1691

PREFACE

Everyone knows that the kingdom of Judah was composed of the two tribes of Judah and Benjamin, and that the ten other tribes who revolted against Rehoboam comprised the kingdom of Israel. As the kings of Judah were of the house of David, and had as part of their territory the town and temple of Jerusalem, all the priests and Levites withdrew with them, and remained always attached to them. Because, since the temple of Solomon had been built, sacrifices were no longer allowed elsewhere; and all those other altars which were raised to God on mountains, for that reason called in Scripture the high places, were not acceptable to him. So the legitimate religion no longer existed anywhere but in Judah. The ten tribes, apart from a very small number of persons, were either idolators or schismatics.

Moreover, these priests and these Levites themselves formed a very numerous tribe. They were divided into various groups to serve in turn in the temple, from one sabbath day to the next. The priests were of the family of Aaron; and it was only those of that family who could perform sacrifices. The Levites were subordinate to them, and were responsible for, among other things, the singing, the preparation of sacrifices, and guarding the temple. This name of Levite is none the less sometimes given indiscriminately to the whole tribe. Those who were on duty had, like the high priest, their lodging in the porticoes or galleries with which the temple was surrounded, and which formed part of the temple itself. The whole edifice was generally known as the Holy Place. But this name was given more particularly to that part of the inner temple where there were the golden candlesticks, the altar of incense, and the tables where the shew-bread was laid. And this part was distinguished again from the Holy of Holies, where the ark was, and which only the high priest had the right to enter, once a year. There was a fairly continuous tradition that the mountain on which the temple was built was the same mountain on which Abraham had once offered his son Isaac as a sacrifice.

I thought I should explain these particulars, so that those who are not sufficiently familiar with Old Testament history are not brought up short in reading the tragedy. The subject of the play is the recognition of Joash and the placing of him on the throne; and I should properly have entitled it *Joash*. But since most people have heard of the piece only by the name *Athaliah*, I thought it would be inconvenient to present it to them under another title; besides, Athaliah plays so important a role in it, and the piece ends with her death. The following are some of the principal events which preceded this great action.

Joram, king of Judah, son of Jehoshaphat, and the seventh king of David's line, married Athaliah, daughter of Ahab and Jezebel, who reigned in Israel and were both famous—but especially Jezebel—for their bloody persecutions against the prophets. Athaliah, not less ungodly than her mother, soon dragged the king her husband into idolatry, and even had a temple to Baal—who was the god of the country of Tyre and Sidon, where Jezebel was born—built in Jerusalem. Joram, having seen all the princes, his children, with the exception of Ahaziah, perish at the hands of Arabs and Philistines, himself died miserably of a long disease which consumed his bowels. His terrible death did not stop Ahaziah imitating his ungodliness and that of Athaliah his mother. But this prince, having reigned for only a year, while paying a visit to the king of Israel, Athaliah's brother, was involved in the ruin of the house of Ahab, and was killed by order of Jehu, whom God had had consecrated by his prophets to rule over Israel and be the minister of his vengeance. Jehu exterminated all the posterity of Ahab, and had Jezebel thrown out of the window so that, in accordance with Elijah's prophecy, she was eaten by the dogs in the vineyard of that same Naboth whose death she had once encompassed in order to seize his inheritance. Athaliah, having heard in Jerusalem of all these massacres, decided that for her part she would exterminate entirely the royal line of David by killing all the children of Ahaziah, her grandchildren. But happily Jehosheba, Ahaziah's sister and Joram's daughter—by a mother other than Athaliah—arriving while the throats of the princes her nephews were being cut, found a way of extracting from among the dead the little Joash who was still sucking, and confided him, with his nurse, to the high priest, her husband, who hid both of them in the temple, where the child was brought up secretly till the day when he was proclaimed king of Judah. The Book of Kings says this was seven years later. But the Greek text of the Book of Chronicles, which Sulpicius Severus followed, says it was eight years. It is this which allows me to make the prince nine or ten, to put him in the position to answer the questions he is asked.

I do not think I have made him say anything which would be above the capacity of a child of this age who had intelligence and a good memory. But even if I have gone a little beyond that point, it has to be considered that this is a quite extraordinary child, brought up in the temple by a high priest who, regarding him as the only hope of his nation, had instructed him early in all the duties of religion and of kingship. It was not the same with the children of the Jews as it is with most of ours. They were taught the holy scriptures, not only as soon as they had reached the age of reason, but, to use St Paul's expression, 'from a child'. Every Jew was under an obligation to write out the whole volume of the law in his own hand, once in his lifetime. Kings were even obliged to write it out twice, and they were enjoined to have it continually before their eyes. I may say that France sees in the person of a prince of eight and a half, who is today its chief delight, an illustrious example of what can be done by good natural endowments, helped by an excellent education; and that if I had given the little Joash the same discernment which shines out in the replies this young prince gives, I should rightly have been accused of having sinned against the laws of probability.

The age of Zechariah, the son of the high priest, not being mentioned, he may, if one wishes, be supposed to be two or three years older than Joash.

I have followed the explanation of several very able commentators who prove, from the scriptural text itself, that all those soldiers to whom Jehoiada, or Joad, as he is called in Josephus, distributed the arms consecrated to God by David, were all priests and Levites, as were the five captains who commanded them. As these commentators say, everything in so holy an action should be holy, and no profane person should be employed in it. It was not a question merely of keeping the sceptre in the house of David, but of preserving the line of descendants of that great king from which the Messiah was to be born. 'For this Messiah, so often promised as a son of Abraham, was also to be the son of David and of all the kings of Judah.' So it is that the illustrious and learned prelate from whom I have borrowed these words calls Joash the precious remnant of the house of David. Josephus speaks of him in the same terms. And the scriptures expressly say that God did not exterminate the whole of Joram's family, wishing to save for David the lamp he had promised him. And what else was this lamp than the light which was one day to be revealed to the nations?

History does not specify on which day Joash was proclaimed. Some commentators assert that it was a feast day. I have chosen that of Pentecost, which was one of the three great feasts of the Jews. The publishing of the law on Mount Sinai was celebrated then, and the first bread of the new harvest was there offered to God, on which account it was also known as the feast of the first-fruits. I thought that these circumstances would provide some variety for the songs of the chorus.

This chorus is composed of young girls of the tribe of Levi, and I put at the head of them a girl I represent as the sister of Zechariah. It is she who brings the chorus to her mother's residence. She sings with them, speaks for them, and in short carries out the functions of the personage who, in the classical choruses, was called the Coryphaeus. I have also tried to imitate from the ancients that continuity of action which ensures that their stage never remains empty, the divisions between the acts being marked only by the hymns and reflections of the chorus, which are related to what is happening.

It may be I shall be thought to have been a little bold in having dared to bring on to the stage a prophet inspired by God, and one who predicts the future. But I have taken the precaution of putting into his mouth only expressions drawn from the prophets themselves. Although Scripture does not say in express terms that Jehoiada had the spirit of prophecy, as it does in the case of his son, it represents him as a man filled with the spirit of God. And besides does it not appear from the gospel that he could prophesy in his capacity as high priest? I suppose therefore that he sees in his mind the fatal change in Joash, who, after thirty years of a very godly reign, gave himself over to the evil counsels of flatterers, and made himself unclean by the murder of Zechariah, the son and successor of the high priest. This murder, committed in the temple, was one of the principal causes of the anger of God against the Jews, and of all the evils which occurred to them afterwards. It is even suggested that from that day on all the oracles of God in the sanctuary ceased. It is this which gave me occasion for the prophecy by Jehoiada, immediately afterwards, of both the destruction of the temple and the ruin of Jerusalem. But as the prophets generally add consolations to their threats, and because, besides, it is a question of putting on the throne one of the ancestors of the Messiah, I have taken the opportunity of giving a glimpse of the coming of this comforter, for whom all the just of ancient times longed. This scene, which is a kind of episode, naturally calls for music, in view of the fact that several prophets were accustomed to enter into their moments of inspiration to the sound of instruments. As witness this troop of prophets who came before Saul with harps and lyres which were carried before them, and as witness Elisha himself, who being consulted about the future by the king of Judah and by the king of Israel, said, as Jehoiada does here: 'But now bring me a minstrel.' Add to that that this prophecy does much to increase the confusion at this point, by the consternation and the different movements it causes in the chorus and the principal actors.

THE CHARACTERS

JOASH, king of Judah, son of Ahaziah, known as ELIAZIN

ATHALIAH, widow of Joram, grandmother of Joash

JEHOIADA, the high priest

JEHOSHEBA, Joash's aunt, wife of the high priest

ZECHARIAH, son of Jehoiada and Jehosheba

SALOMITH, sister of Zechariah

ABNER, one of the chief officers of the kings of Judah

AZARIAS, ISHMAEL, and the three other leaders of the priests and Levites

MATTAN, an apostate priest, who performs sacrifices to Baal

NABAL, Mattan's confidant

HAGAR, waiting-woman to Athaliah

A band of priests and Levites—Athaliah's attendants—Joash's nurse—Chorus of girls of the tribe of Levi

The scene is in the temple, in Jerusalem, in a hall in the high priest's apartment.

ACT I

SCENE 1

Jehoiada, Abner

ABNER

Yes, I am here to worship the Eternal
In his temple, according to old usage,
With you to celebrate the famous day
When, on Mount Sinai, we were given the Law.
How times have changed! As soon, once, as the return   5
Of this day sounded on the sacred trumpet,
The holy people would come flooding in
The temple doors; everywhere were festoons,
And all went in procession to the altar,
Their hands full of the produce of their fields,   10
First-fruits which they would consecrate to God.
There were never enough priests for the sacrifices.
Now one rash woman has upset all this
And turned these bright days into days of darkness.
It is much now if a small group of worshippers   15
Dares to retrace some outline of the past.
The rest flaunt their forgetfulness of God,
Or even, crowding round the altars of Baal,
Would be instructed in his shameful mysteries,
Blaspheming the one name their fathers invoked.   20
I fear that Athaliah—to hide nothing from you—
Will have you dragged away from the altar
And so consummate her deadly revenge,
Removing the last traces of forced respect.

JEHOIADA

What is it gives you these dark forebodings?   25

ABNER

Do you think you can be just and go scot-free?
She has long enough hated this rare courage
Which, with Jehoiada, adds lustre to the mitre.*
She has long treated your love for religion

As if it signified disloyalty and revolt.   30
Jealous as she is of any striking merit,
The queen hates most of all your wife Jehosheba.
If Jehoiada is heir of the high priest Aaron,
Jehosheba is the sister of our last king.
Besides, Mattan, that sacrilegious priest,   35
Worse than Athaliah, lays siege to her;
Mattan, who shamefully forsook our altars
And showed great zeal in persecuting virtue.
What matter though, crowned with a foreign head-dress,
This Levite serves as minister of Baal?   40
The temple beckons him, and his impiety
Would bring to nothing the God he has deserted.
To ruin you he invents a thousand tricks.
Sometimes he pities you, often even praises you;
He assumes a false air of gentleness;   45
As if to mask the blackness of his humour,
He sometimes tells the queen you are to be feared,
Sometimes, seeing her insatiable love of gold,
He pretends that, in a place you alone know,
You are concealing treasures amassed by David.   50
Finally, for the last two days proud Athaliah
Has seemed as if buried in some dark concern.
I watched her yesterday, and saw her eyes
In fury as they surveyed the holy place,
As if, in the depth of this vast edifice,   55
God hid an armed avenger who would punish her.
The more I think of it, the less I doubt
That it is on you that her anger will break,
And that the bloodthirsty daughter of Jezebel
Will come to attack God even in his sanctuary.   60

JEHOIADA

He who can curb the fury of the waves
Can also foil the plots of wicked men.
Obedient always to his holy will,
I fear God, Abner, and have no other fear.
And yet I thank you for the attentive zeal   65
Which so opens your eyes to all my dangers.
I see that in your heart you hate injustice,
That you are still an Israelite indeed.

Heaven be blessed! But does this secret anger,
This virtue that does nothing, satisfy you?   70
Can faith without action be sincere?
For more than eight years now an impious foreigner
Has usurped all the rights of David's sceptre,
And with impunity bathed in the blood of our kings;
The detestable murderer of her son's children,   75
She even raises her treacherous hand against God.
And you, a pillar of this tottering state,
You, brought up in the camp of Jehoshaphat,
Who under his son Joram commanded our armies,
Who alone reassured our frightened towns   80
When once the sudden death of Ahaziah
Scattered his whole camp in the face of Jehu:
'I fear God,' you say, 'his truth touches me.'
This is how God answers you by my mouth:
'Why pretend to a zeal for my law?   85
You think to honour me with barren vows?
What fruit have I of all your sacrifices?
Do I have need of the blood of goats and heifers?
The blood of your kings cries out, and no one listens.
Break, break all compact with impiety.   90
Exterminate the crimes among my people,
Then you will bring me sacrifices indeed.'

ABNER
Ah, what can I do, with this enfeebled race?
Benjamin has no strength, Judah no virtue.
The day they saw their kingly line extinguished   95
Extinguished also all their ancient courage.
'God himself', they say, 'has abandoned us.
Formerly so jealous of the Hebrews' honour,
He is indifferent now to their great fall
And at the last his pity is exhausted.   100
No longer do we see his powerful hands
Strike terror by innumerable miracles.
The sacred ark is dumb, and speaks no more oracles.'

JEHOIADA
And what time ever was so teeming with wonders?
When did God show his power more abundantly?   105

So, have you still eyes to see nothing,
Ungrateful race! What, can so many miracles
Strike on your ears without touching your hearts?
Must I, Abner, must I recall the history
Of the famous prodigies accomplished in our days?   110
The public shaming of the tyrants of Israel,
And God found faithful in accomplishing his threats;
The impious Ahab destroyed, his blood soaking*
The very field he had usurped by murder;
Jezebel sacrificed near this fatal field,   115
This queen trampled under the horses' hooves;
The dogs licking up her inhuman blood,
The limbs of her foul body torn apart;
The whole troop of lying prophets confounded,
And flames from heaven called down upon the altar;*   120
Elijah confidently commanding the elements,
Closing the heavens and turning them to bronze,
And the land three years without rain or dew,
The dead brought back when Elisha spoke:*
Recognize, Abner, by these marvellous signs,   125
A God the same today as in all ages.
When he will, he can produce his glory;
His people is forever in his mind.

ABNER

But where are the honours so promised to David,*
And foretold also to Solomon his son?   130
Alas, we hoped that from their happy race
Would issue an unending line of kings,
That over every tribe and every nation
One of them would forever be established,
Would everywhere make war and discord cease   135
And see all the kings of the earth at his feet.

JEHOIADA

Why do you not accept heaven's promises?

ABNER

This king of David's line, where shall we find him?
Can heaven itself repair this ruined tree,
Dried up and withered to its very roots?   140
Athaliah stifled the child in its cradle.

Do the dead rise up from the tomb after eight years?
Ah! had she, in her fury, been mistaken,
If some drop of our kings' blood had escaped ...

JEHOIADA
Well, what would you do then?

ABNER
　　　　　　　　　Oh happy day!　　　　　145
With what joy then would I acknowledge my king!
Can you doubt that our tribes would fall at his feet?
But why flatter my hopes with such vain thoughts?
The pitiful heir of these triumphant kings,
Ahaziah was left alone with his children.　　　150
I saw the father pierced by Jehu's arrows,
You saw the son massacred by the mother.

JEHOIADA
I speak in riddles. But, when the star of day
Has done a third of its course from east to west,
When the third hour calls everyone to prayer,　　155
Be in the temple, with your present zeal.
God will then show you, by his mighty benefits,
That his word does not change or know deceit.
Go, for I must prepare for this great day;
Already the dawn whitens the temple roof.　　160

ABNER
I do not understand this talk of benefits.
Noble Jehosheba is on her way to you.
I will go now and join the faithful troop
Attracted by this day of solemn pomp.

SCENE 2

Jehoiada, Jehosheba

JEHOIADA
The time has come, princess, and we must speak;　　165
Your fortunate theft can be hidden no longer.
The culpable insolence of God's enemies,
Making ill use of this profound silence,

Has too long charged him with failing in his promises,
What am I saying? Success has driven them mad;   170
Even on our altar your unjust stepmother
Would offer an idolatrous incense to Baal.
Let us bring forth the young king your hands saved
And brought up in the temple under God's wing.
He will have the courage of our Hebrew kings;   175
Already he has a mind beyond his years.
Before my voice explains his destiny
I will offer him to the God by whom kings reign.
Then at once, assembling our Levites and our priests,
I will proclaim him the heir of their masters.   180

JEHOSHEBA
And are his name and his destiny yet known?

JEHOIADA
He still answers to the name of Eliazin
And thinks himself some child spurned by his mother,
To whom I have acted as father out of pity.

JEHOSHEBA
Alas, from what danger I had saved him!   185
What danger must he now face once more!

JEHOIADA
What! Is your faith already weak and wondering?

JEHOSHEBA
My lord, I yield at once to your wise counsels.
From the day I snatched the child from his death
I put his fate entirely in your hands.   190
Even, fearing the violence of my love,
As much as I could I have avoided him,
Lest when I saw him some frail indiscretion
Might let fall tears which would reveal my secret.
And I have thought myself in duty bound   195
To consecrate these three whole days and nights
Entirely to weeping and to prayers.
Yet today can I put a question to you?
What friends have you ready to second you?
Will the brave Abner come to our defence?   200
Has he sworn that he will stand by his king?

JEHOIADA

   Though Abner's loyalty may be relied upon,
   He does not yet know whether we have a king.

JEHOSHEBA

   To whom have you entrusted Joash's safety?
   Has Obed or has Amnon now this honour?   205
   The benefits that my father showered upon them ...

JEHOIADA

   Yet both have been corrupted by Athaliah.

JEHOSHEBA

   Whom do you then set against her creatures?

JEHOIADA

   Have I not told you? There are the priests and Levites.

JEHOSHEBA

   I know that you have secretly gathered them round you,   210
   Far-sightedly doubling their numbers; filled as they are
   With love for you and horror of Athaliah,
   They are bound in advance by a solemn oath
   To this son of David we are to reveal to them.
   But, burn as they may with a noble ardour,   215
   Can they by themselves avenge their king's quarrel?
   Is their zeal enough, for such an enterprise?
   Do you doubt that Athaliah, at the first hint
   That a son of Ahaziah is within the walls,
   Will not collect her proud foreign cohorts,   220
   Surround the temple and break down the doors?
   Then will your holy ministers be enough,
   Raising their innocent hands to the Lord,
   They who can only lament and pray for our crimes
   And have shed no blood but that of their sacrifices?   225
   In their arms, perhaps, Joash, pierced by blows ...

JEHOIADA

   Do you reckon God nothing? Yet he works for us.
   God, who protects the orphan in his innocence
   And causes his power to shine out in the weak;
   God, who hates tyrants, and who in Jezraël,   230
   Swore to exterminate Ahab and Jezebel;
   God who, striking Joram, their daughter's husband,*

    Has pursued their family even in his son;
    God, whose avenging arm, for a time suspended,
    Is always stretched out on this impious race?   235

JEHOSHEBA
    It is his justice visited on all these kings
    That I fear for my unfortunate brother's son.
    Who knows whether this child, in the wake of their crime,
    Was not, like them, condemned from his birth?
    Whether God, setting him apart from an odious race,   240
    Will wish to pardon him for David's sake?
        Alas! his horrible condition when heaven gave him to me
    Comes back to me always, and fills my mind with dread.
    The room was full of princes with their throats cut:
    A dagger in hand, the merciless Athaliah   245
    Was inciting her barbarous soldiery to carnage
    As she pursued her train of assassination.
    Left for dead, Joash suddenly caught my eye.
    I can still see his poor distracted nurse,
    Who had vainly thrown herself in the murderer's way   250
    And held him feebly clasped against her breast.
    I took him up, all bloody. Bathing his face,
    My tears brought back some trace of feeling to him;
    And, either still in fear, or trying to caress me,
    I felt myself pressed by his innocent arms.   255
    Great God! may my love not be fatal to him!
    He is the precious remnant of the faithful David.
    Brought up in your house, in the love of your law,
    He still knows of no other father but you.
    If, on the point of attacking a murderous queen,   260
    My faith grows fearful at the sight of danger,
    If flesh and blood, which are today so troubled,
    Have too large a share in the tears I shed for him,
    Preserve the heir of your holy promises,
    And punish only me for all my weakness.   265

JEHOIADA
    There is nothing criminal in your tears, Jehosheba.
    But God wills us to hope in his fatherly care.
    He does not seek, blinded by his anger,
    The father's impiety in the son who fears him.

All the Hebrews who still remain faithful　　　270
Will come this day to renew their vows to him.
Great as the respect is for David's line,
There is as much hatred of Jezebel's daughter.
Joash will move them by his noble modesty,
In which the glory of his blood shines through;　　275
And God, supporting our conduct with his voice,
Will speak close to their hearts in his temple.
Two faithless kings in turn have braved his anger:
Now there must be a king upon the throne
Who will one day recall how God raised him up　　280
To his ancestral place by the hand of his priests,
By whose hand too he was brought back from the dead,
And David's torch, once put out, was relighted.
　　Great God, if you foresee that he unworthily
Will not pursue the course that David set,　　285
May he be like the fruit which falls unformed
Or which a hostile breath dries in the flower,
But if this same child, as a willing pupil,
Is to be the instrument of your designs.
Grant that the sceptre pass to the right heir.　　290
Deliver his powerful enemies into my hands,
Weak as they are, and confound the cruel queen's counsels.
Deign, deign, my God, to pour upon Mattan
And upon her, that rash and erring spirit
Which is the fatal precursor of the fall of kings.　　295
　　The time is short. Goodbye. Your son and his sister
Bring you the daughters of the holiest families.

SCENE 3

Jehosheba, Zechariah, Salomith, Chorus

JEHOSHEBA

Dear Zechariah, go without delay,
Accompany your august father's footsteps.
　　And you, young faithful troop of the daughters of Levi,　　300
In whose hearts God has lit the fire of his zeal,
And who so often come to share my sighs,

Children, my only joy in my long troubles;
Those festoons in your hands, those flowers on your heads,
Were once the proper ornaments of our festivals.   305
But alas! in this time of shame and grief,
What offering is more fitting than our tears?
I hear already, I hear the sacred trumpet,
And soon the temple doors will be thrown open.
While I go to prepare our procession,   310
Sing, praise the God you have come here to seek.

SCENE 4

The Chorus

ALL

The universe is full of his magnificence:
Adore him and invoke him evermore,
This God, whose empire is before time was.
Sing, publish all his benefits.   315

A VOICE [*alone.*]

In vain would unjust violence
Silence the praise his people give him:
His name will never perish.
One day proclaims his glory to the next.
The universe is full of his magnificence.   320
Sing, publish all his benefits.

ALL

The universe is full of his magnificence.
Sing, publish all his benefits.

A VOICE [*alone.*]

He gives the flowers their darling colours.
He brings the fruits to birth and ripens them,   325
Dispensing in accordance with their need
The warmth by day, the coolness of the night;
The earth returns them to him multiplied.

ANOTHER VOICE

He bids the sun impart its animation;
Its light falls as a gift from his hands.   330

And yet his pure and holy law
Is the best gift he gives to humankind.

ANOTHER

Mount Sinai, O preserve the memory
Of that for ever great and famous day*
When, on your flaming top, 335
Wrapped in a heavy cloud the Lord let shine
On mortal eyes a sparkle of his glory.
O tell us why
These fires, this lightning,
Torrents of smoke, this crackling in the air, 340
These trumpets and this thunder?
Was it to overthrow the order of the elements
That he made himself manifest?
Was it to shake the earth to its foundations?

ANOTHER

He came to show the children of the Hebrews 345
The changeless light of his divine precepts.
He came to bid his people
To love him with an everlasting love.

ALL

O divine, O pleasing law!
O justice, O supreme goodness! 350
How reasonable, how sweet it is
To pledge our love and fealty to this God!

A VOICE [*alone.*]

He saved our fathers from a heavy yoke,
Nourished us in the desert with his bread.
He gives us laws, he gives himself: 355
It is for this he bids us love him.

ALL

O justice, O supreme goodness!

THE SAME VOICE

For them he parts the sea and makes dry land,
And from a barren rock makes waters flow.
He gives us laws, he gives himself: 360
It is for this he bids us love him.

ALL

> O divine, O pleasing law!
> How reasonable, how sweet it is
> To pledge our love and fealty to this God!

ANOTHER VOICE [*alone.*]

> You who know only servile fear,   365
> Ungrateful, can so kind a Lord not please you?
> And are your hearts so hard you cannot love him?
> Is it so difficult?
> The slave must fear a tyrant's rage,
> But children find their share of love.   370
> You would have God load you with benefits,
> Yet never love him!

ALL

> O divine, O pleasing law!
> How reasonable, how sweet it is
> To pledge our love and fealty to this God!   375

ACT II

SCENE 1

Jehosheba, Salomith, Chorus

JEHOSHEBA

Enough, my daughters! Interrupt your hymns.
It is time we took our part in public prayers.
Now is the moment. Let us go, and celebrate
The great day and appear before the Lord.

SCENE 2

Zechariah, Jehosheba, Salomith, Chorus

JEHOSHEBA

But what do I see? My son, what brings you back?   380
Where are you running, pale and out of breath?

ZECHARIAH

O mother!

JEHOSHEBA

Well, what is it?

ZECHARIAH

The temple profaned!

JEHOSHEBA

What?

ZECHARIAH

And the altar of the Lord abandoned!

JEHOSHEBA

I tremble. Tell your mother what has happened.

ZECHARIAH

The high priest, father, in accordance with the law,   385
Had just offered to God, who feeds us all,
The first loaves from the grain of the new harvest,
And was presenting, in his bloodstained hands,
The smoking entrails of his pacific victims.

Standing beside him, young Eliazin,⠀⠀⠀⠀⠀⠀⠀⠀⠀390
With me, was serving in his linen robe;
And meanwhile, the priests were sprinkling with the blood
Of sacrificed flesh, altar and congregation.
There was a confused noise and the people, surprised,
Suddenly turned away their eyes and thoughts.⠀⠀⠀⠀395
A woman . . . Can she be named without blasphemy?
A woman . . . It was Athaliah herself.

JEHOSHEBA

Heaven!

ZECHARIAH

⠀⠀⠀⠀⠀Into one of the courts reserved for men
This proud woman went with head held high,
And was about to cross even the boundaries⠀⠀⠀⠀400
Of the sacred precincts permitted only to Levites.
The people were terrified and scattered everywhere.
Father . . . Ah, how angry his looks were!
Moses appeared less terrifying to Pharaoh.*
'Queen,' he said, 'leave this formidable place⠀⠀⠀405
From which your sex and impiety exclude you.
Would you brave the majesty of the living God?'
The queen then, with a ferocious glance,
Opened her lips, no doubt to blaspheme.
I do not know, perhaps the angel of God⠀⠀⠀⠀410
Appeared to her and showed a flaming sword;
But her tongue was instantly frozen in her mouth
And all her insolence was beaten down.
Her eyes, as if in terror, dared not move.
Eliazin above all seemed to astonish her.⠀⠀⠀⠀415

JEHOSHEBA

What then? Has she seen Eliazin?

ZECHARIAH

We were both looking at the cruel queen,
And both our hearts were struck with equal horror.
But the priests suddenly surrounded us.
We were sent out. I do not know what followed,⠀⠀⠀420
And I came to tell you of these disasters.

JEHOSHEBA

Ah! She has come no doubt to take him from us;

And it is he her fury seeks at the altar.
Perhaps at this moment the cause of so many tears ...
Remember David, O God, my help in trouble.   425

SALOMITH
What is the cause of all these tears you shed?

ZECHARIAH
And is the life of Eliazin in danger?

SALOMITH
Does it mean that the queen is angry with him?

ZECHARIAH
What could she fear from a helpless, fatherless child?

JEHOSHEBA
Ah, here she is. Let's go. We must avoid her.   430

SCENE 3

Athaliah, Hagar, Abner

HAGAR
Madam, why do you linger in these places?
Here everything offends and angers you.
Leave this temple to the priests who live in it.
Escape from all this tumult and come to your palace,
To give your troubled mind a little peace.   435

ATHALIAH
No, I cannot: you see me confused and weak.
Go, tell Mattan to come here, and come quickly.
I shall be happy if, with his aid,
I can find the peace I seek, but which eludes me.

[*She takes a seat.*]

SCENE 4

Athaliah, Abner, etc.

ABNER
Madam, forgive me if I dare defend him;   440
Jehoiada's zeal should not have surprised you.

Such is the eternal order of our God.
It was he traced his temple and his altar,
Entrusted his sacrifices to Aaron's line
And prescribed to the Levites their place and offices,   445
Above all, forbade to all their posterity
To have to do with any other god.
You are the wife and mother of our kings,
You surely can be no stranger to our ways?
Do you not know our laws? And must you now …   450
Here is your Mattan, I will leave you with him.

ATHALIAH

Your presence, Abner, is necessary here.
Let us have no more of Jehoiada's insolence,
And all that vain heap of superstition
Which will not admit other nations to your temple.   455
A more urgent question now alarms me.
I know that, brought up to arms from his childhood,
Abner has a noble heart, that he repays
At once what he owes to his God and to his kings.
Stay.

SCENE 5

Mattan, Athaliah, Abner, etc.

MATTAN

           But is this the place for you, great queen?   460
What cares now trouble you, what terror chills you?
What do you come to seek, among your enemies?
And dare you to approach this profane temple?
Have you so put aside your acute hatred …

ATHALIAH

Listen to me, both of you, and attentively.   465
     I do not want, here, to recall the past,
Nor yet to justify the blood I spilt.
What I did, Abner, was what I thought I must do.
I will not take a headstrong people for judge.
Whatever insolence they have dared to utter,   470
Heaven itself has justified my actions.
Brilliant successes have established my power,

Making Athaliah respected from shore to shore.
Have I not given Jerusalem profound peace?
No wandering Arab now prowls by the Jordan,   475
Nor do haughty Philistines, by ceaseless raids,
As in the time of your kings, make its banks desolate;
The Syrian treats me now as queen and sister;
Finally, in my own house the treacherous oppressor,
Who would barbarously have assailed even me,   480
Jehu, the proud Jehu, trembles in Samaria.
Pressed upon all sides by a powerful neighbour
I have raised up against this assassin,
He leaves me sovereign mistress of this country.
I was at peace, enjoying the fruits of my foresight,   485
But in these last days trouble has importuned me,
Interrupting the course of my prosperity.
A dream (and should a dream make me uneasy?)
Has set a gnawing worry in my heart.
    It was in the horror of the blackest of nights.   490
My mother Jezebel appeared before me,
Grandly arrayed as on the day of her death.
All her misfortunes had left her pride untouched.
Her looks had still even that borrowed splendour
With which she used to paint and trick out her face   495
To make good the irreparable damage of age.
'Tremble,' she said to me, 'true daughter that you are.
The cruel God of the Jews will beat you too.
I pity you falling into his fearful hands,
My daughter.' As she concluded her awful words,   500
Her ghost appeared to bend over my bed.
And I, who stretched out my hands to embrace her,
Found nothing there except a horrible mixture
Of bones and blood and, still covered in muck,
Rags that were soaked in blood, ghastly arms and legs   505
Which the dogs had fought over as they devoured them.

ABNER
  Great God!

ATHALIAH
            In this disorder my eyes saw
  A young child covered in a shining robe

Such as one sees the priests of the Hebrews dressed in.
The sight of him revived my appalled spirits.   510
But when, recovering from my mortal despair,
I was admiring his noble and modest bearing,
I felt all at once a murderous blade
Which the traitor plunged deep into my heart.
This strange concurrence of such different objects   515
May seem to you to have been the work of chance.
For some time I myself, ashamed of my fear,
Took it to be the effect of hysteria.
But this memory has so far obsessed me
That in my sleep I have twice seen the same thing.   520
Twice my sad eyes have seen this same child,
And always he was trying to run me through.
At last, tired of the horrors which pursued me,
I went to pray to Baal for protection,
And sought repose at the foot of his altars.   525
What cannot terror do to a mortal mind!
An instinct drove me to the temple of the Jews,
And I conceived the idea of appeasing their God.
I thought to assuage his anger with gifts,
So that this God, be who he may, would be gentler.   530
Pontiff of Baal, excuse my infirmity.
I went in. The people fled. The sacrifice stopped.
The high priest advanced on me in fury.
As he spoke to me, I was surprised and terrified
To see this same child who had threatened me,   535
Just as I saw him in my horrible dream.
I saw him, looking the same, the same linen robe,
The way he walked, his eyes, and all his features.
It is he. He was walking beside the high priest,
But soon they made him disappear from view.   540
You see what trouble it is that keeps me here,
And why I wanted to consult you both.
    Mattan, what does this prodigy foretell?

MATTAN
    This dream, and this account of it, are terrifying.

ATHALIAH
    But this fatal child, Abner, you saw him.   545

What is he? Of what blood, and of what tribe?

ABNER

There were two children serving at the altar.
One is Jehoiada's son, his mother is Jehosheba.
The other I do not know.

MATTAN

Why deliberate?
Madam, you must make sure of them both.   550
You know my regard for Jehoiada,
And that I do not seek to avenge my wrongs;
Justice alone determines my advice;
But after all, were it his own son,
Would he himself wish a guilty life spared?   555

ABNER

Of what crime can a child be capable?

MATTAN

Heaven has shown him with a dagger in his hand.
Heaven is just and wise, and does nothing in vain.
What more do you ask for?

ABNER

Is believing a dream
Warrant enough for bathing in a child's blood?   560
You do not yet know who was his father,
What he is.

MATTAN

He is feared, that is enough.
If his parents are indeed illustrious,
Such distinction should bring his end the sooner.
If he happens to come from the common people,   565
What does it matter if such blood is spilt?
Is it for kings to hesitate in their justice?
Their safety often depends upon quick punishment.
Let us not hinder them by scruples of that kind.
Whomever they suspect is no longer innocent.   570

ABNER

Come, Mattan, is that how a priest should talk?
I, brought up in war to all the horrors of carnage,
The rigorous minister of royal vengeance,

It is I who speak for the unfortunate here.
And you, who should feel for him as a father,   575
You, who should serve peace in times of anger,
Concealing your resentment under a false zeal,
To your mind the blood does not flow fast enough!
    You asked me to speak without deception,
Madam. What is it then which is so much feared?   580
A dream, a feeble child, your accusing eye
Thinks, perhaps wrongly, that it has recognized.

ATHALIAH

I am willing to believe, Abner, that I was mistaken.
Perhaps I have made too much of an empty dream.
Well, I must see this child at closer quarters   585
And study his features more at my leisure.
Let both of them appear in my presence.

ABNER

I fear . . .

ATHALIAH

            Does this not show a lack of acquiescence?
What reason could there be for this strange refusal?
It could give me suspicions I never had.   590
Let Jehosheba, I say, or Jehoiada bring them.
I can, when I wish, speak as your sovereign.
Your priests, I freely admit it, Abner,
Have cause to think Athaliah generous.
I know that they allow themselves the licence.   595
Of talking freely about me and against me.
Yet they still live, their temple still stands.
But I feel that my patience is exhausted.
Jehoiada should moderate his zeal;
Let him not anger me by a second outrage.   600
Go.

SCENE 6

Athaliah, Mattan, etc.

MATTAN

    Now at last I can speak freely to you.

I can show the truth in the plain light of day.
Some monster is coming to birth in this temple,
Queen: do not wait until the cloud bursts.
Abner was with the high priest before daybreak.   605
You know his love for the blood of his kings.
And who knows whether Jehoiada would not substitute,
In place of them, the child heaven troubles you with,
Either his own son, or some other . . .

ATHALIAH
                                        You open my eyes.
Yes, I begin to see heaven's warning clearly.   610
But I want still to be delivered from my doubt.
A child cannot well conceal what he thinks.
Often a word will betray a great design.
Let me see him, dear Mattan, and question him.
You, meanwhile, go, and do not raise the alarm   615
But see that all my Tyrians have their weapons.

SCENE 7

*Joash, Jehosheba, Athaliah, Zechariah, Abner, Salomith,
two Levites, Chorus, etc.*

JEHOSHEBA [*to the two Levites.*]
O you, the Lord's ministers, be ever watchful;
Keep these dear, precious children in your sight.

ABNER [*to Jehosheba.*]
Princess, have no anxiety, I will guard them.

ATHALIAH
O heavens! the more closely I look at him,   620
It is he. Horror has seized all my faculties.
Wife of Jehoiada, is this your son?

JEHOSHEBA
Who? Him, madam?

ATHALIAH
                        Him.

JEHOSHEBA
                                I am not his mother.

That is my son.

ATHALIAH

> And you, who is your father?
Answer me now, child.

JEHOSHEBA

> Heaven till this day...   625

ATHALIAH

Why are you so in haste to answer for him?
It is for him to speak.

JEHOSHEBA

> At so young an age,
What explanation can you hope to have?

ATHALIAH

This age is innocent. It is ingenuous
And does not yet alter the simple truth.   630
Let him explain all that concerns himself.

JEHOSHEBA [quietly.]
Great God, deign to grant his lips wisdom.

ATHALIAH

What are you called?

JOASH

> They call me Eliazin.

ATHALIAH

Your father?

JOASH

> They say I am an orphan,
Thrown into God's arms from the day of my birth,   635
And I never knew who my parents were.

ATHALIAH

You have no parents?

JOASH

> They have abandoned me.

ATHALIAH

How? And since when?

JOASH

> Ever since I was born.

ATHALIAH
Is it not known at least what your country is?

JOASH
This temple is my country; I know no other.   640

ATHALIAH
Where do they say that they happened to find you?

JOASH
Among cruel wolves who were about to eat me.

ATHALIAH
Who put you in this temple?

JOASH
                          An unknown woman,
Who gave no name, and has not since been seen.

ATHALIAH
In your first years, whose hands took care of you?   645

JOASH
Did God ever abandon his children in need?
He gives the little birds their daily food,
And his goodness extends to the whole creation.
Every day I invoke him, and with fatherly care,
He feeds me from the gifts brought to his altar.   650

ATHALIAH
What new prodigy troubles and embarrasses me?
The sweetness of his voice, his childhood, grace,
Make my hostility give way insensibly
To ... Can it be I am feeling pity?

ABNER
Madam, you see this terrible enemy.   655
It can be seen now that your dreams were lies,
Unless it be that this pity which disturbs you
Could be the fatal blow that made you tremble.

ATHALIAH [to Joash and Jehosheba.]
You are going?

JEHOSHEBA
                You have heard his fortune.
His presence could become importunate.   660

ATHALIAH
  No. Come back. What do you do every day?

JOASH
  I worship the Lord. They explain the law to me.
  They teach me to read in his holy book,
  And already I am trying to write it out.

ATHALIAH
  What does it tell you, this law?

JOASH
                  That God wants our love,   665
  That sooner or later he will avenge himself
  On all those who blaspheme his holy name;
  That he is the defender of the timid orphan;
  That he resists the proud, and punishes murder.

ATHALIAH
  I understand. But the people shut up here,   670
  What do they do all day?

JOASH
              Praise God and bless him.

ATHALIAH
  God wants men always to pray and contemplate?

JOASH
  All profane exercise is banished from his temple.

ATHALIAH
  What pleasures have you then?

JOASH
  I serve the high priest with incense or salt.   675
  I hear songs of God's infinite greatness.
  I see the splendid order of his ceremonies.

ATHALIAH
  And have you no pleasanter pastimes than that?
  I pity the sad fate of a child like you.
  Come to my palace, there you will see my glory.   680

JOASH
  What, should I there forget God's benefits?

ATHALIAH
  No, I would not constrain you to forget them.

JOASH

You do not pray to him.

ATHALIAH

But you can pray.

JOASH

And at the same time see another invoked?

ATHALIAH

I have my God, and serve him; you will serve yours.　685
They are two powerful gods.

JOASH

Mine must be feared.
He only is God, madam; yours is nothing.

ATHALIAH

With me, there would be all sorts of pleasures.

JOASH

The joy of the wicked passes like a torrent.

ATHALIAH

Who are the wicked, then?

JEHOSHEBA

Madam, excuse　690
A child . . .

ATHALIAH [to Jehosheba.]

I like to see how you instruct him.
Certainly, Eliazin, you knew how to please me.
No doubt you are no ordinary child.
You see, I am the queen, and I have no heir.
Take off that garment, give up this poor trade.　695
I want you to have a share of all my wealth.
From today, try the effect of my promises.
At my table, everywhere, sitting beside me,
I intend to treat you as my own son.

JOASH

As your son?

ATHALIAH

Yes. You say nothing?

JOASH

But what　700
A father I should leave! And for . . .

ATHALIAH

Well?

JOASH

Such a mother!

ATHALIAH [*to Jehosheba.*]
His memory is good, and in all he says
I read the minds of you and Jehoiada.
See how, infecting his gullible youth,
You two employ the calm I leave you in.   705
You are encouraging them to hate and fury.
You pronounce my name to them only with horror.

JEHOSHEBA
Can our misfortunes be concealed from them?
The whole world knows. You yourself glory in it.

ATHALIAH
Yes, my just anger, I am proud of it,   710
Has avenged my family on my own posterity.
So, I have seen my father and brother murdered,
My mother thrown from the walls of the palace,
And in the same day seen all those throats cut
—What a horror to see!—twenty-four kings' sons.   715
And why? To avenge I know not what prophets
Whose indiscreet fury she had punished.
And I, a heartless queen, an unloving daughter,
Slave of a cowardly and a frivolous pity,
I should not at least have repaid this blind rage   720
With murder for murder and with outrage for outrage,
And treated all the posterity of your David
As the unhappy sons of Ahab were treated?
Where should I be now if, overcoming my weakness,
I had not choked back a mother's tenderness;   725
If, pouring out torrents of my own blood,
My hand had not thus suppressed your plots?
Finally the implacable vengeance of your God,
Entering our houses, has broken all friendship.
I regard David with horror, and that king's sons,   730
Although born of my blood, are foreigners to me.

JEHOSHEBA
You have succeeded! May God see, and judge us.

ATHALIAH
This God, who has long been your only refuge,
What will become now of what he predicted?
Let him give you this king promised to all nations,   735
The son of David who is your certain hope . . .
But we shall meet again. Goodbye, I am happy:
I wanted to see, I have seen.

ABNER [to Jehosheba.]
                     And as I promised,
I give you back this child you entrusted to me.

SCENE 8

Jehoiada, Jehosheba, Joash, Zechariah, Abner, Salomith,
Levites, Chorus

JEHOSHEBA [to Jehoiada.]
You heard what this proud queen said, my lord?   740

JEHOIADA
I heard it all, with pity for what you felt.
These Levites and I were ready to help you,
And even resolved to die with you if need be.

         [To Joash, embracing him.]

May God watch over you; your courage, child,
Has borne a noble witness to your name.   745
Abner, I shall not forget this crucial service.
Do not omit to appear when I am expecting you.
And we, our eyes sullied, our prayers interrupted
By the intrusion of this profane and murderous woman,
Let us go in, and let the pure blood I shed   750
Cleanse even the marble which her feet have touched.

SCENE 9

The Chorus

ONE OF THE GIRLS
What star has newly lighted up our eyes?

What will this marvellous child one day become?
He braves the ostentation of the haughty,
And does not yield   755
To all its dangerous shows.

ANOTHER

Many there are eager to cense
The altar of Athaliah's god;
But one courageous child makes known
The true God is alone eternal,   760
And speaks out like a new Elijah
Before another Jezebel.

ANOTHER

Who will reveal your secret birth,
Dear child? Are you some holy prophet's son?

ANOTHER

You grow up as sweet Samuel grew*   765
In the shadow of the tabernacle
To be the Hebrews' hope and guide.
May you console Israel as Samuel did.

ANOTHER [sings.]

Blessed a thousand times
The child whom the Lord loves,
Who early hears his voice   770
And whom God deigns to instruct as his own!
Brought up far from the world, with all heaven's gifts
He is embellished from his birth;
The sullying approach of the wicked   775
Leaves him untouched and innocent.

THE WHOLE CHORUS

Happy, oh happy is the childhood
Of him the Lord instructs and will defend!

THE SAME VOICE [alone.]

As in a secret valley,
Beside a crystal stream,   780
A budding lily, nature's darling,
Grows sheltered from the blast of the north wind,
Brought up far from the world, with all heaven's gifts
He is embellished from his birth;

The sullying approach of the wicked   785
Leaves him untouched and innocent.

THE WHOLE CHORUS
Happy a thousand times,
The child the Lord makes docile to his laws!

ONE VOICE [*alone.*]
My God, that such a budding virtue
Should walk uncertainly amidst such perils!   790
That a soul seeking you, desiring innocence,
Should find his purposes impeded!
How many enemies assail him!
Where can your saints then hide?
Sinners possess the earth.   795

ANOTHER
Palace of David, his dear city,
O famous mountain God himself inhabited,
How have you called the wrath of heaven upon you?
Zion, dear Zion, what do you say, who see
An impious foreigner   800
Seated, alas, upon the throne of your kings?

THE WHOLE CHORUS
Zion, dear Zion, what do you say, who see
An impious foreigner
Seated, alas, upon the throne of your kings?

THE SAME VOICE [*continues.*]
Instead of pleasing hymns,   805
Such as your David sang in holy joy,
Blessing his God, his Lord, his father,
Zion, dear Zion, what do you say, who see
Praise given to the impious foreigner's god
And the name that your kings adored, blasphemed?   810

ONE VOICE [*alone.*]
How long, O Lord, how long must we behold
The wicked in rebellion against you?
They brave you even in your holy temple,
And call our people's adoration, madness.
How long, O Lord, how long must we behold   815
The wicked in rebellion against you?

ANOTHER

What use to you is this uncivil virtue?
They ask, for here are pleasures to be had.
Why run from their enjoyment?
Your God does nothing for you.   820

ANOTHER

This impious troop says: Let us laugh and sing!
Let our desires roam as they will
From flowers to flowers, one pleasure to the next;
Madness it is, to trust the future.
Who knows the number of our fleeting years?   825
Let us enjoy life while we can, today:
Who is sure of existence on the morrow?

THE WHOLE CHORUS

Let them weep, O my God, and shake with fear,
Those whose unhappy lot is not to see
The eternal splendour of your holy city.   830
It is for us to sing, it is to us
The light of life eternal is revealed;
It is for us to sing your gifts and greatness.

ONE VOICE [*alone.*]

What will remain of all these empty pleasures
Into which they plunge their souls? A dream gone by,   835
The falsity of which is seen at last.
When they awake, O waking full of horror!
While the poor at your table
Will taste your peace, and joy unspeakable,
They will in fear drink of the bottomless cup   840
You will put to the lips, in the day of wrath,
Of all the guilty race.

THE WHOLE CHORUS

O waking full of horror!
O dream that does not last!
O dangerous error!   845

ACT III

SCENE 1

Mattan, Nabal, Chorus

MATTAN

Go, you girls, and say to Jehosheba
That Mattan wants to speak to her in private.

ONE OF THE GIRLS

Mattan! May he incur the wrath of heaven!

NABAL

So! They have disappeared without replying to you?

MATTAN

Let us approach.

SCENE 2

Zechariah, Mattan, Nabal

ZECHARIAH

                              You are rash! Where are you going?   850
Take care not to advance beyond this point.
The holy ministers of God live here.
The laws forbid all entry to the profane.
Whom do you seek? My father, this solemn day,
Avoids the criminal sight of foul idolaters;   855
My mother, now prostrate before the Lord,
Fears to be interrupted in that duty.

MATTAN

We will wait, my son; you need not be concerned.
It is to your illustrious mother I wish to speak.
I am here charged with an order from the queen.   860

SCENE 3

Mattan, Nabal

NABAL

Even their children have their haughty airs.
But what does Athaliah want to do?
How is it that her plans are so confused?
Offended this morning by Jehoiada's insolence,
And fatally threatened by a child in a dream,   865
She was to have vented her anger on Jehoiada
And hand the temple over to Baal and you.
You had already told me of your joy,
And I hoped for my share of this rich prey.
What is it makes her so changeable and irresolute?   870

MATTAN

My friend, these last two days she has not been herself.
She is no longer that bold, enlightened queen,
So far superior to her timid sex,
Who used to surprise her enemies and crush them,
And knew the cost of letting the moment pass.   875
Fear of remorse now troubles her great soul;
She drifts and hesitates, like any woman.
I had but newly filled with bitter resentment
That heart, already no stranger to heaven's threats.
She had herself, relying on me for vengeance,   880
Told me without delay to assemble her guard.
But, either because this child, brought before her,
Said to be an unfortunate spurned by his parents,
Had diminished the terrifying effect of her dream,
Or because she had found something attractive in him,   885
I found her anger hesitant and uncertain,
Putting off her revenge to another day.
All her plans appeared mutually destructive.
'I have found out for what this child is destined,'
I said. 'They are boasting now about his ancestors.   890
Jehoiada from time to time shows him off
To the disaffected, and suggests to the Jews
That they should look to him as another Moses;

This he backs up with lying oracles.'
These words at once brought colour to her cheek.   895
There never was a lie that worked so quickly.
    'Is it for me to weaken and hesitate?
Let us', she said, 'throw off this agitation.
Inform Jehosheba of the decision yourself:
The fires will be lit, the swords are in readiness.   900
Nothing can now prevent the sack of the temple
Unless I have this child as a hostage.'

NABAL

Well, will they, for a child they do not know,
One perhaps thrown into their arms by chance,
Wish to see their temple, buried under the grass . . .   905

MATTAN

Ah, but you do not know the proudest of mortals.
Before Jehoiada will deliver that child
He has himself consecrated to his god,
You will see him suffer the most terrible of deaths.
Besides, their attachment to this child is clear.   910
If I understand the queen's narrative aright,
Jehoiada knows more than he says about its birth.
Be it what it may, that child will prove fatal.
They will not part with him. I shall do the rest;
And I hope that sword and fire will rid my eyes   915
Finally of the sight of that odious temple.

NABAL

What can inspire you with so deep a hatred?
Are you carried away by your zeal for Baal?
I am descended from Ishmael, as you know,
And serve neither Baal nor the God of Israel.   920

MATTAN

My friend, do you suppose a frivolous zeal
For a vain idol, would blind such as I?
For a fragile piece of wood which, despite my efforts,
The worms eat every day upon the altar?
Born a minister of the God adored in this temple,   925
Mattan perhaps would be his servant still,
If a passion for greatness, a thirst for command,
Could somehow bear the constriction of his yoke.

Is it necessary, Nabal, to recall to your mind
The famous quarrel between Jehoiada and me,   930
When I dared to dispute his right to the censer,
My intrigues, battles, my tears, my despair?
He beat me, and I took up another career,
And gave my mind completely to the court.
Gradually I rose to have the ear of kings   935
And soon my voice became an oracle.
I studied their hearts, flattered their every whim;
I scattered flowers on the edge of precipices;
Beside their passions, nothing was sacred to me;
I changed my principles to suit their taste.   940
While the inflexible stubbornness of Jehoiada
Gave such offence to their effeminate ears,
I always managed to charm them by my skill,
Hiding the unpleasant truth from their eyes,
Giving a favourable colour to all their furies;   945
Above all, reckless with the blood of the losers.

Finally, Athaliah had a temple built
To the new god whom she had introduced.
Jerusalem wept to see itself profaned.
All the children of Levi, in consternation,   950
Raised frightful cries to heaven, at the event.
I alone, as an example to the timid Hebrews,
Having deserted their law, approved the enterprise,
And so won the right to be the priest of Baal.
By that I made myself terrible to my rival;   955
I wore the tiara, had an equal place in processions.
Yet I confess, even at the height of my glory,
The nagging memory of the God I left
Still throws a trace of terror into my soul.
This is what drives me on and feeds my fury.   960
Happy if, taking a full revenge on his temple,
I can at last show that his hatred is powerless
And, amidst the wreckage, ravages, and death,
Can in these outrages shed my last remorse.
But here is Jehosheba.

SCENE 4

Jehosheba, Mattan, Nabal

MATTAN

                Sent by the queen   965
To re-establish calm and dissipate hatred,
Princess, in whom heaven put so gentle a spirit,
It will not surprise you that I come to you.
A rumour, which I suspected was a lie,
Supported by warnings she received in a dream   970
About Jehoiada, accused of conspiracy,
Was about to unleash the full flood of her anger.
I do not want to boast here of my services.
Jehoiada has been unjust to me, I know,
But we must repay offences with benefits.   975
I came anyhow charged with pacific words.
Live, solemnize your festivals as you will.
She demands only one pledge of your obedience:
It is—and I have done my best to dissuade her—
This orphan child she says that she has seen.   980

JEHOSHEBA
Eliazin!

MATTAN
            She makes me slightly ashamed.
Perhaps she gives too much weight to an idle dream;
But you will declare yourselves her mortal enemies
If this child is not put into my hands at once.
The queen impatiently awaits your answer.   985

JEHOSHEBA
So that is the peace she sends you to announce!

MATTAN
Could you for one moment hesitate to accept it?
Is it dear at the price of a little compliance?

JEHOSHEBA
I wondered whether Mattan, giving up his tricks,
Could have overcome the injustice of his heart,   990

And whether one who had devised so many evils
Could be the author of some shadow of good.

MATTAN

What are you complaining of? Have I come in a fury
To snatch your son Zechariah from your arms?
Who is this other child you hold so dear?   995
It is my turn to be surprised, that you care so much for him.
Is he so extraordinary a treasure for you?
Is it a liberator heaven is preparing?
Think. Your refusal might confirm for me
A rumour that is beginning to circulate.   1000

JEHOSHEBA

What rumour?

MATTAN

                    That this child is from a great house;
That your husband plans some great destiny for him.

JEHOSHEBA

And Mattan, by this rumour which well suits his fury . . .

MATTAN

Princess, it is for you to disabuse me.
I know that, her hatred of lies being implacable,   1005
Jehosheba would sacrifice her own breath,
If the price of it were as much as a single word
Against what she sincerely knew to be truth.
Is there really no trace of where this child comes from?
Nothing but obscurity concerning his race?   1010
You yourself do not know who his parents were?
From what hands Jehosheba took him up?
Speak, I am listening, and ready to believe you.
Princess, give glory to the God you serve.

JEHOSHEBA

How can you honestly dare to name   1015
A God about whom you teach only blasphemies?
And how can you bear witness to his truth,
You who preside in an infected pulpit
Where lies prevail and spread their poison round,
You, fed upon deceits and upon treason?   1020

SCENE 5

Jehoiada, Jehosheba, Mattan, Nabal

JEHOIADA
Where am I? Is this not the priest of Baal?
What, daughter of David, you are talking to the traitor?
You let him talk to you? And do not fear
That, from the gulf half-open at his feet,
Flames may not issue at once to consume you,   1025
Or that these walls may not fall on him and crush you?
What does he want, this enemy of God,
Impudently infecting the air we breathe here?

MATTAN
This virulence is like Jehoiada.
He would do well to show a little prudence,   1030
To respect a queen, and not to insult
Him she has deigned to charge with her commands.

JEHOIADA
Well then, what evil tidings does she have for us?
What frightful order comes by such a hand?

MATTAN
I have told Jehosheba what her will is.   1035

JEHOIADA
Out of my sight then, monster of impiety!
Go, let your horrors overflow upon us.
God will settle you with the rest of your perjured race,*
Abiram and Dathan, Doeg, Achitophel.
The dogs, to whom his arm delivered Jezebel,   1040
Are waiting for his wrath to be visited on you;
Already they bark at your door and demand their prey.

MATTAN [*in some confusion.*]
Before the end of the day . . . you will see which of us . . .
Is to . . . But let us go, Nabal.

NABAL
                                    Are you lost?
What is it makes you act so erratically?   1045
This is the way.

SCENE 6

Jehoiada, Jehosheba

JEHOSHEBA
     The storm is about to break.
Athaliah is furious and demands Eliazin.
Already they are beginning to guess the mystery
Of his birth, and of your plans, my lord.
Mattan came near to saying who his father was.   1050

JEHOIADA
Who has revealed this to the perfidious Mattan?
Has your confusion not told Mattan too much?

JEHOSHEBA
I did what I could to remain mistress of myself,
But, believe me, my lord, the danger is close now.
Let us preserve this child for happier times.   1055
While the evil-doers are deliberating,
Before they surround him, before they snatch him from us,
Allow me once again to conceal him.
The door and roads still remain open.
Must he be taken into the grimmest deserts?   1060
I am ready. I know a secret way out,
By which, without them seeing him, undetected,
Crossing the torrent of Cedron, taking him with me,
I will go into the desert where, once, weeping,
And like us seeking to find safety in flight,   1065
David escaped from a rebellious son.
I should fear lions and bears less for his sake ...
But why refuse the assistance of Jehu?*
It may be that this is something you had not thought of.
Let us ask Jehu to look after this treasure.   1070
He could be taken into Jehu's states today,
And the road which leads there is not a long one.
Jehu's heart is not fierce and inexorable;
And David's name has favour in his eyes.
Alas! is there a king so hard and cruel,   1075
Unless his mother were another Jezebel,

That he would not have pity on such a suppliant?
Is his cause not common to all kings?

JEHOIADA

What timid counsels are you daring to suggest?
Could you see hope in the support of Jehu?   1080

JEHOSHEBA

Does God forbid all care and thought for the future?
Is he not offended by excessive confidence?
Does he not use men for his holy purposes?
Did he not himself put arms in Jehu's hands?

JEHOIADA

Jehu, who was chosen by his divine wisdom,   1085
Jehu, on whom I see you set your hopes,
Has repaid his benefits by forgetting them.
Jehu leaves Ahab's terrible daughter in peace,
Follows the profane example of the kings of Israel,
Has preserved the temple of the foul god of Egypt.   1090
Jehu, who dares to offer in the high places
A blasphemous incense which God cannot allow,
Has neither the upright heart nor the pure hands
To serve his cause and to avenge his wrongs.
No, no, we must rely on God alone.   1095
Let us show Eliazin and, far from hiding him,
Let his head be circled by the royal diadem.
My will is rather to advance the set hour,
Before Mattan has completed his designs.

SCENE 7

*Jehoiada, Jehosheba, Azarias, followed by the Chorus
and several Levites*

JEHOIADA

Well, Azarias, so the temple is closed?   1100

AZARIAS

I have seen all the doors closed myself.

JEHOIADA

No one but you and your holy company left?

AZARIAS

    I have twice inspected all the sacred courts.
    All have fled; they have gone beyond recall,
    A wretched flock of sheep, scattered by fear;   1105
    God is now served only in his holy tribe.
    No terror equal to this has struck this people
    Since it escaped out of Pharaoh's hands.

JEHOIADA

    A race of cowards indeed, and born for slavery,
    Bold only against God! Our task must go on.   1110
    But who has charge now of the children we have here?

ONE OF THE GIRLS

    Ah, could we, Lord, cast ourselves off from you?
    Or are we strangers in the temple of God?
    You have with you our fathers and our brothers.

ANOTHER

    Alas! if to avenge the shame of Israel,   1115
    Our hands cannot as once those of Jael did,
    Transpierce the impious heads of God's enemies,
    We can at least sacrifice our lives.
    When your arms fight to save the temple,
    He can at least be invoked by our tears.   1120

JEHOIADA

    See what avengers arm themselves for your quarrel!
    Eternal wisdom, here are priests and children!
    But if you are at their side, who can dislodge them?
    When you will you can call us back from the tomb.
    You strike, you cure; you kill and bring to life.   1125
    They take no comfort in their own merits
    But in your name, on which they have called so often,
    And your promises sworn to the holiest of their kings
    In this temple where you make your sacred dwelling,
    And which should last as long as the sun itself.   1130
    But why does my heart now quake in holy dread?
    Is this the divine spirit taking possession of me?
    It is he. He warns me: he speaks; my eyes are opened
    And the dark centuries ahead are visible.
    O Levites, pour your harmonies upon me   1135
    To keep time with the movements which transport me.

[*The* CHORUS *sings to the accompaniment of the whole symphony of instruments.*]

> Now let the voice of God be heard,
> And his divine oracle be to our hearts
> As to new grass in spring
> The coolness of the dew is in the morning   1140

JEHOIADA

Heavens, listen to my voice; and earth, give ear.
Say no more, Jacob, that your Lord is sleeping.
Sinners, be seen no more: the Lord awakes.

[*Here the symphony begins again, and at the same time Jehoiada continues his speech.*]

How is pure gold changed into common lead?*
Who is the pontiff slain in this holy place?   1145
Weep, O Jerusalem, weep, perfidious city,
The unhappy murderer of his holy prophets!
Your God has put aside his love for you.
Your incense, in his eyes, is a foul incense.
    Where do you lead these women and these children?*   1150
The Lord has now destroyed the queen of cities.
His priests are captive and his kings rejected;
God now invites none to his celebration.
Cast yourself down, temple; cedars, spurt flames.
    I grieve for you, Jerusalem;*   1155
Whose hand this day has stolen all your charms?
Who will make of my eyes two springs of tears
    To weep for your ill state?

AZARIAS

O holy temple!

JEHOSHEBA

                    David!

CHORUS

                    God of Zion,
Recall your ancient kindness, and be favourable.   1160

[*The symphony begins again, and Jehoiada interrupts it after a moment.*]

JEHOIADA

What new Jerusalem,*

Brilliant with lights, now issues from the desert,
And bears upon her brow an immortal seal?
     Sing, peoples of the earth.
More pleasing and more lovely, now Jerusalem   1165
     Is born again.
And whence come all these children, from all sides,
Children she did not carry in her womb?
Jerusalem, raise your proud head aloft;
See all the kings, astonished by your glory: 1170
The kings of all the nations fall before you,
     Kiss the dust of your feet.
Peoples vie with each other for your light.
Happy those who will feel their souls on fire
          With holy care for Zion!   1175
          Heavens, spread your dew,
     And may the earth bring forth its Saviour.

JEHOSHEBA

Alas! from whence will come this signal favour,
If the kings from whom the Saviour is to descend . . .

JEHOIADA

Make ready the rich diadem, Jehosheba,   1180
Which David bore upon his sacred brow.

[To the Levites.]

To be armed, you must follow me through these precincts,
Where there is hidden, far from profane eyes,
The formidable pile of swords and lances
Which were once tempered by the blood of Philistines: 1185
The victorious David, loaded with years and honours,
Consecrated them to the God who had protected him.
Could they be used for a more noble purpose?
Come, and I will myself distribute them.

SCENE 8

Salomith, Chorus

SALOMITH

What fears, my sisters, and what mortal troubles!   1190
     Almighty God, are these the first-fruits,
          The perfumes and the sacrifices
     That should this day be offered on your altars?

A GIRL

  What a sight for our timid eyes!
   Who would have thought   1195
  We should see bloody swords and murderous lances
   Flash in the house of peace?

ANOTHER

How can Jerusalem, indifferent to her God,
Be silent amidst all these pressing dangers?
  How can it be, sisters, that, to protect us 1200
Brave Abner at least does not speak a word?

SALOMITH

Alas, in a court which has no other laws
  Than force and violence,
  Where honours and employments
Are the reward of blind and base obedience, 1205
  My sisters, who would speak
  For mourning innocence?

ANOTHER

And in this peril, this extreme confusion,
For whom is the sacred diadem made ready?

SALOMITH

  The Lord has deigned to speak,   1210
  But what he has revealed to his prophet
   Who will make clear to us?
   Is it for our defence he arms?
    Or is it to crush us?

ALL [sing.]

O promise! Menace! Obscure mystery!   1215
How many ills and benefits, in turn,
Are prophesied! And yet how, with so much anger,
  Can so much love be reconciled?

ONE VOICE [alone.]

Zion will be no more: a cruel flame
  Will destroy all her beauties.   1220

ANOTHER VOICE

God protects Zion, which is founded
  On his eternal word.

THE FIRST
I see his brightness disappear from my sight.

THE SECOND
I see his light spread everywhere.

THE FIRST
Zion has sunk into a pit.   1225

THE SECOND
Her brow is towering in the heavens.

THE FIRST
How low has she fallen!

THE SECOND
                                How she has risen in glory!

THE FIRST
How many cries of pain!

THE SECOND
                                What songs of victory!

A THIRD
Let us no more be troubled: our God some day
        Will unveil this great mystery.   1230

ALL THREE
        Let us revere his anger;
        Hope in his love.

ANOTHER
        Can the peace of a heart
        Which loves you, O my God, ever be troubled?
        Your supreme will is all it seeks,   1235
                Never itself.
        On the earth, even in heaven,
        Can there be any other happiness
                Than the calm peace
Of a heart which is full of love for you?   1240

ACT IV

SCENE 1

Joash, Jehosheba, Zechariah, Salomith, a Levite, Chorus

SALOMITH

Majestically, walking beside my mother,
Little Eliazin comes, my brother with him.
Sisters, what are they carrying, under those veils?
And what can that sword be, which is borne before them?

JEHOSHEBA [*to Zechariah.*]

My son, place respectfully on this table   1245
The formidable book of our holy law.
And you too, gentle Eliazin, place
This august diadem near the holy book.
Levite, you must—Jehoiada so orders—
Put the sword of David there beside his crown.   1250

JOASH

Princess, what is this unaccustomed show?
Why the holy book, the sword, the diadem?
Since first the Lord received me into his temple,
I have not seen the like of this displayed.

JEHOSHEBA

Your doubts, my son, will soon be all cleared up.   1255

JOASH

You want to try the diadem on my brow?
Ah, princess, take care not to profane its glory.
Respect the memory of the king who wore it.
An unfortunate child abandoned to the bears . . .

JEHOSHEBA [*trying the diadem on him.*]

Allow me, son, I do as I am commanded.   1260

JOASH

But yet I hear sobs from your parted lips!
Princess, you are weeping! Why this touch of pity?
Is it that today, presented as a sacrifice,
I must, as happened once to Jephtha's daughter,*

Appease the wrath of the Lord by my death?   1265
Alas! all a son has belongs to his father.

JEHOSHEBA

Here comes one who will tell you what heaven wills.
Fear nothing. And the rest of us must go.

SCENE 2

Jehoiada, Joash

JOASH [running into the arms of the high priest.]
Father!

JEHOIADA

       Well, son?

JOASH

             What are these preparations for?

JEHOIADA

It is right, my son, that I should declare it.   1270
You must now be informed, before them all,
Of God's designs for his people and for you.
You must be armed with courage and new faith:
Now is the time to show that ardent zeal
It has been my care to cultivate in your heart,   1275
And to pay to God all that you owe to him.
Are you disposed to be so nobly generous?

JOASH

I am ready to give my life, if he wills it.

JEHOIADA

The story of our kings has been read to you often:
Do you recall, my son, what strict prescriptions   1280
A king fit to be crowned has to comply with?

JOASH

A wise king, so God himself has pronounced,
Does not put his trust in silver and gold;
He fears the Lord his God, and keeps before him
His precepts, laws, and his severe judgments,   1285
And does not crush his brothers with unjust burdens.

JEHOIADA

But if you had to model yourself on one of them,
Which of these kings, my son, would you choose?

JOASH

David, full of a faithful love of the Lord,
Seems to me the most proper pattern to follow.   1290

JEHOIADA

You would not imitate in their excesses
Unfaithful Joram, impious Ahaziah?

JOASH

O father!

JEHOIADA

      Finish, say what is in your mind.

JOASH

May any who resembles them so perish!

      [Jehoiada throws himself at his feet.]

Father, why are you doing that before me?   1295

JEHOIADA

I am paying you the respect I owe to my king.
Joash, be worthy of your forefather David.

JOASH

I, Joash?

JEHOIADA

      You will learn by what signal grace
God, thwarting the intentions of a furious mother,
When her dagger was already in your heart,   1300
Chose you, and saved you from the midst of the slaughter.
You have not yet made your escape from her rage:
In the same blaze of anger in which once
She tried to kill you, the last of her son's children,
She is cruelly intent upon your death now,   1305
And is still pursuing you under your disguised name.
But already I have called to your standards
An obedient people prompt to avenge you.
    Enter, you generous heads of the sacred families
Which are in turn honoured with the holy ministry.   1310

SCENE 3

Joash, Jehoiada, Azarias, Ishmael, and the three other chiefs of the Levites

JEHOIADA [*continues.*]
    King, these will avenge you against your enemies.
    Priests, this is the king I promised you.

AZARIAS
    What! It is Eliazin?

ISHMAEL
                 What, this lovely child . . .

JEHOIADA
    Is the true heir of the kings of Judah,
    The last-born child of sad Ahaziah   1315
    Who, as you know, was given the name of Joash.
    Like you, all Judah, pitying the destiny
    Of this so tender flower, so soon cut down,
    Thought he had met the fate of his dead brothers.
    He was like them struck by a treacherous knife.   1320
    But God was able to mitigate the blow,
    Preserved the trace of warmth still in his heart,
    Allowed Jehosheba to trick the murderers
    And carry him off, all bloody, in her bosom,
    Then, with only me as her accomplice,   1325
    To hide both child and nurse in the temple.

JOASH
    Alas! father, how shall I ever repay
    So much love, so many benefits received?

JEHOIADA
    Keep your gratitude for another time.
       Here is your king, the only hope you have.   1330
    My care has kept him from you till this day:
    Ministers of the Lord, complete your work.
    At any moment Jezebel's murderous daughter,
    Informed that Joash still sees the light of day,
    Will come to thrust him back into the tomb.   1335
    Already, not knowing him, she would cut his throat.

Holy priests, you must prevent her rage.
Have done with the shameful slavery of the Jews,
Avenge your dead princes, revive your law;
See that the two tribes recognize their king.   1340
The task no doubt is great and dangerous.
I am attacking a haughty queen on her throne,
One under whose banners a numerous army
Marches, insolent foreigners and faithless Hebrews.
But my strength is in God, whose interest guides me.   1345
Remember that all Israel is in this child.
Already this avenging God begins to trouble her.
Already, in spite of her, I have brought you together.
She thinks we have no arms here, and no defence.
Let us crown and proclaim Joash without delay.   1350
Then, as intrepid soldiers of the new prince,
Let us march, relying on battle for the decision;
And, waking the faith slumbering in men's hearts,
Seek out our enemy even in her palace.

     And what hearts so plunged in a cowardly sleep,   1355
Seeing us advancing in this holy array,
Will not hasten to follow our example?
A king raised in the temple by God himself,
The successor of Aaron, followed by his priests,*
Leading the children of Levi into battle,   1360
And, in those same hands which the people revere,
The arms David consecrated to the Lord?
God will spread terror among his enemies.
Bathe in the infidel blood without horror.

     Strike both the Tyrians and Israelites.   1365
Are you not descended from those famous Levites
Who, when in the desert fickle Israel
Was wickedly praying to the god of the Nile,
In holy zeal destroyed their dearest relations
And consecrated their hands in the faithless blood,   1370
So by this noble exploit acquiring the honour
Of being the only ones to serve the Lord's altars?

     But I see you are already on fire to follow me.
Swear then, above all, and on this holy book,
To live, to fight, to die for this king   1375
Whom heaven gives back to you on this very day.

AZARIAS

Yes, we swear, for ourselves, for all our brothers,
To set Joash again on his ancestors' throne,
And not to lay down the arms we have been given
Until we have taken revenge on all his enemies. 1380
If any transgressor in any way fails this promise,
May he, great God, feel your avenging fury;
May he and his children, excluded from your heritage,
Be in the ranks of the dead you will know no more.

JEHOIADA

And, king, will you not swear to be always faithful 1385
To that law which is your eternal rule?

JOASH

Could I act otherwise than by the law?

JEHOIADA

My son, I dare still call you by that name,
Bear with this tenderness, forgive the tears
Which my just fears for you force from me now. 1390
Brought up far from the throne, from this fatal honour,
Alas, you do not know the poisoning charm,
The intoxication of absolute power,
Or the seductive talk of flatterers.
Soon they will tell you that the holiest laws, 1395
Which rule the common people, obey kings;
That nothing can check a king but his own will;
That he should sacrifice everything to his greatness;
That the people is condemned to toil and tears,
And needs a rod of iron to govern it; 1400
That, if not oppressed, it will become the oppressor.
And so from snare to snare, from pit to pit,
Corrupting the pleasing purity of your life,
Finally they will bring you to hate the truth,
Will give you a repulsive impression of virtue. 1405
Alas, they have misled the best of kings.
  Promise on this book and before these witnesses
That God will always be your first concern;
That, severe with the wicked, and the refuge of the good,
You will take God for judge between the poor and yourself; 1410
Remembering, my son, that disguised in this robe,
You were poor like them and like them an orphan.

JOASH

I promise to observe what the law commands.
Punish me, my God, if I abandon you.

JEHOIADA

Come, you must be consecrated with the holy oil.   1415
Appear, Jehosheba; you can show yourself.

SCENE 4

*Joash, Jehoiada, Jehosheba, Zechariah, Azarias, etc., Salomith,
Chorus*

JEHOSHEBA [*embracing Joash.*]

O king, son of David!

JOASH

                    O my only mother!
Come and embrace your brother, Zechariah.

JEHOIADA [*while they are embracing.*]

So, children, may you always be united!

JEHOSHEBA, to *Joash.*

You know then to what blood you owe your life?   1420

JOASH

And what hand, but for you, would have destroyed it.

JEHOSHEBA

So I can call you by your name, Joash.

JOASH

And never will Joash stop loving you.

CHORUS

What! that is . . .

JEHOSHEBA

                    Joash.

JEHOIADA

                         Attend to this Levite.

SCENE 5

Joash, Jehosheba, Jehoiada, etc., a Levite

A LEVITE

There is some design against God, I do not know what;   1425
But on all sides the threatening bronze is echoing;
Fires have appeared, shining amidst the banners;
And Athaliah no doubt is collecting her army.
Already every route to help is closed.
Already the sacred hill where the temple stands   1430
Is invested everywhere by insolent Tyrians.
One of them, blaspheming, has just told us
That Abner is in irons, he can do nothing.

JEHOSHEBA [to Joash.]

Dear child, whom heaven gave back to me in vain,
Alas, I have done what I could to save you.   1435
But God no longer remembers your father David.

JEHOIADA [to Jehosheba.]

What! are you not afraid to draw down his anger
On you and on this king that is so dear to you?
And if God, snatching him finally from your arms,
Willed that the house of David became extinct,   1440
Are you not here upon his holy mountain
Where Abraham raised an obedient arm,
Without a murmur, over his innocent son,
And laid on the faggot this fruit of his old age,
Leaving it to God to accomplish his promise,   1445
And sacrificing to him, with this loved son,
The last surviving hope of his own line?
        Friends, let us split up. Let Ishmael take charge
Of all the side which looks towards the east.
You, where the bear points and you, take the west;   1450
You, the south. Let no one, through excess of zeal
Revealing my plans, neither priest nor Levite,
Emerge before due time or rush forward:
In short let everyone, as one man,
Guard to the death the position I have placed him in.   1455
The enemy is watching us, in his blind rage

Like some poor herd of cattle intended for slaughter,
And thinks to find nothing here but confusion and fear.
Let Azarias accompany the king everywhere.

[*To Joash.*]

Come, dear new offshoot of a valiant race;   1460
Fill your defenders with a fresh audacity.
Come and wear your diadem before their eyes;
At least die as a king, if you must die.

[*To a Levite.*]

Jehosheba, follow him. You, give me these weapons.
Children, offer to God your innocent tears.   1465

SCENE 6

Salomith, Chorus

THE WHOLE CHORUS [*sings.*]
> Children of Aaron, now depart,
> Never did more illustrious quarrel
> Give courage to your ancestors.
> Children of Aaron, now depart.
It is your king, your God, for whom you fight.   1470
ONE VOICE [*alone.*]
> Where are the bolts you hurl,
> Great God, in your just wrath?
> Are you no more the jealous God?
> No more the God of vengeance?

ANOTHER
Where, God of Jacob, is your ancient mercy?   1475
> With horrors all around us,
Do you hear nothing now but our transgressions?
> Are you no more the God who forgives?
THE WHOLE CHORUS
Where, God of Jacob, is your ancient mercy?
ONE VOICE [*alone.*]
> It is at you that, in this war,   1480
> The arrows of the wicked aim:

'Now let us end', they say,
'God's festivals on earth.
Let us deliver mortals from his wearying yoke;
Massacre his holy ones, overthrow his altars;   1485
And of his name and glory
Blot out all recollection;
Let him reign here no more; no, nor his Christ.'

THE WHOLE CHORUS

Where are the blost you hurl,
Great God, in your just wrath?   1490
Are you no more the jealous God,
No more the God of vengeance?

ONE VOICE [*alone.*]

Sad remnant of our kings,
Dear and last flower from a lovely stalk,
Alas, shall we see you a second time   1495
Fall to the knife of a cruel mother?
Amiable prince, tell us, was there some angel
Defended you in your cradle against your murderers?
Or, in the darkness of the tomb
Did the voice of the living God revive your ashes?   1500

ANOTHER

Are the crimes of a father and a grandfather
Who turned against you, imputed now to him?
And is your pity finally withdrawn?

CHORUS

Where, God of Jacob, is your ancient mercy?
And are you no more the God who forgives?   1505

ONE OF THE GIRLS [*not singing.*]

Dear sisters now, do you not hear
The sound of the cruel Tyrians' trumpet?

SALOMITH

Shuddering with horror,
I hear even the shouts the barbarous soldiers make.
Let us run, take refuge in   1510
The salutary shadow
Of the dread sanctuary.

ACT V

SCENE 1

Zechariah, Salomith, Chorus

SALOMITH

Dear Zechariah, what have you to tell us?

ZECHARIAH

Redouble your instant prayers to the Lord.
It may be we are now at our last hour.   1515
The terrible battle, sister, is about to begin.

SALOMITH

What is Joash doing?

ZECHARIAH

              Joash has just been crowned.
The high priest has anointed him with the oil.
O heaven! How joyfully all eyes lit up
At the sight of this king brought back from the dead!   1520
Sister, you can still see the marks of the knife.
His faithful nurse has also appeared now;
She was hidden in a corner of this vast edifice
Where she kept this precious treasure, no one knew how
Except our mother and the Lord our God.   1525
Our Levites wept for joy and tenderness,
Sobbing as they uttered cries of delight.
Amidst all this he was charming, no trace of pride;
He gave his hand to one, kind looks to another,
Swore to be governed by their honest advice,   1530
And called them all his fathers or his brothers.

SALOMITH

Has this secret been spread around outside?

ZECHARIAH

The secret is still confined within the temple.
The children of Levi have been split into groups,
Mustered in profound silence behind the doors.   1535
They are all to rush out at the same time,
Giving the signal by shouting: 'Long live King Joash!'

But father will not let the king risk himself;
He has told Azarias to stay and guard him.
Meanwhile Athaliah, a dagger in her hand,   1540
Is laughing at the weak defence our bronze doors offer.
She is waiting for deadly engines to smash them down,
And meanwhile panting for blood and destruction.
Some priests, sister, first of all proposed
That at least our sacred ark should be put away   1545
In a safe vault dug out by our forefathers.
'An unworthy fear!' father said, 'an insult!
So the ark, which brought down so many proud towers*
And forced the Jordan to turn back in its course,
Triumphing so often over the gods of the nations,   1550
Is to flee at the sight of an insolent woman?'
Mother, who was by the king, in mortal confusion,
Her eyes now on the king and now on the altar,
Said nothing; she gave way under all these alarms,
And would have drawn tears even from the cruellest eyes.   1555
The king from time to time hugged her in his arms,
Spoke kindly to her . . . Dear sister, follow me now,
And, if our king has to die today,
Let us go, let us all suffer the same fate.

SALOMITH
What insolent hand is that, knocking again?   1560
What makes the Levites run in such confusion?
Why this precaution? They are hiding their arms.
Is the temple forced open?

ZECHARIAH
                              Forget your fears.
God is sending us Abner.

SCENE 2

*Abner, Jehoiada, Jehosheba, Zechariah, Salomith, Ishmael, two
Levites, etc.*

JEHOIADA
                              Can I believe my eyes,
Dear Abner? By what route did you arrive here,   1565

Coming through a camp which besieges us all round?
They were saying that Ahab's sacrilegious daughter
Had, to make sure of her inhuman projects,
Loaded your generous hands with shameful irons.

ABNER

Yes, my lord, she feared my zeal and my courage.   1570
But that was the least her rage had in store for me.
Imprisoned by her orders in a horrible dungeon,
I was waiting until, with the temple reduced to ashes,
And all those rivers of blood not yet assuaged,
She came to set me free from a burdensome life   1575
And to cut short days which the grief of surviving my king
Should already have brought to an end a thousand times.

JEHOIADA

By what miracle did you obtain your pardon?

ABNER

God alone knows what passed in that cruel mind.
She sent for me, and with an uncertain air   1580
She said: 'You see my soldiers all round the temple.
An avenging fire will soon reduce it to ashes,
And your God will not be able to defend it against me.
His priests can still—but they will have to be quick—
Redeem it if they comply with two conditions: 1585
That, with Eliazin, they put in my hands
A treasure which I know they know about,
One formerly amassed by your King David,
And left under vow of secrecy to the high priest.
Go, tell them that, at this price, I will let them live.   1590

JEHOIADA

What course, dear Abner, do you think we should follow?

ABNER

All David's gold, if indeed it is true
That you are keeping some secret treasure of David's,
And everything rich and rare that you may have saved
From the grasp of this avaricious queen,   1595
Give it to her. Do you want unclean assassins
To come and smash the altar, burn the cherubim,*
And, laying an insolent hand upon the ark,
Desecrate the sanctuary with your own blood?

JEHOIADA

    But would it be proper, Abner, for generous hearts   1600
    To hand over an unhappy child to his death,
    A child whom God himself entrusted to me,
    And to ransom ourselves at the price of his blood?

ABNER

    Alas! God sees my heart. Would to this powerful God
    That Athaliah should forget an innocent child,   1605
    And her cruelty be content with Abner's life,
    Thinking she could calm the torments of heaven by my death!
    But what can your useless efforts do for him?
    When you all perish, will he perish any the less?
    Is God commanding you to do the impossible?   1610
    Obeying the law of an inflexible tyrant,
    Moses, whose mother abandoned him to the Nile,
    Saw himself condemned to die almost as he was born.
    But God, preserving him against all hope,
    Appointed the tyrant himself to provide for his childhood.   1615
    Who knows what he has in store for Eliazin,
    And whether, preparing a like fate for him,
    He has not already made capable of pity
    The implacable murderess of our unhappy kings?
    At least, and Jehosheba has observed it too,   1620
    I have lately seen her moved by the sight of him;
    I have seen the violence of her anger fall.
    Princess, you remain silent in this danger?
    What! for a child who is a stranger to you,
    Will you allow Jehoiada fruitlessly   1625
    To have his throat cut, yours, your son's, all your people's,
    And the only place on earth where God wants to be worshipped
    Destroyed by fire? What more would you do
    If this child were the last shoot of your ancestral kings?

JEHOSHEBA [aside to Jehoiada.]

    You see his tenderness for the blood of his kings.   1630
    Why do you not speak to him?

JEHOIADA

                         It is not the time.

ABNER

    The time is shorter than you think, my lord.

While you are hesitating about your reply,
Mattan, seething with rage beside Athaliah,
Asks for the word to be given that the slaughter should start.   1635
Must I then throw myself at your sacred feet?
In the name of the holy place only you may enter,
The terrible resting place of God's own majesty,
However hard the terms may seem to you,
Let us think how to ward off this unexpected blow.   1640
Only give me the time to turn round.
Tomorrow, this night even, I will take measures
To safeguard the temple and avenge the sacrilege.
But I can see that my tears and useless talk
Are of little assistance in persuading you;   1645
They make no impression on your severe virtue.
Ah well, find me some weapon, a sword of some kind,
And, at the temple doors, where the enemy waits for me,
Let Abner at least be allowed to die fighting.

JEHOIADA

I give in. I accept what you propose.   1650
Let us, Abner, deflect these threatened evils.
It is true, one of David's treasures remains.
The care of it was entrusted to my fidelity.
It was the last hope of the unhappy Jews,
And faithfully I hid it from the light.   1655
But, since it must be discovered to your queen,
I am going to satisfy her, our doors will open.
Let her come in, attended by her bravest captains,
But let her keep away from our holy altars
The reckless fury of her mob of foreigners.   1660
Spare me the horror of the temple being pillaged.
Could they have any suspicion of priests and children?
Let her bring only a few followers with her.
And as to this child, so feared and so dreaded,
I know, Abner, the rectitude of your heart.   1665
I want to tell you his origins in her presence.
You will see whether we should put him into her power,
And you shall judge between Athaliah and him.

ABNER

My lord, I take him under my protection now.
Fear nothing. I will hurry back to her who sent me.   1670

SCENE 3

Jehoiada, Jehosheba, Ishmael, Zechariah, etc.

JEHOIADA

Great God, this is your hour, they are bringing your prey.
Listen, Ishmael.

[*He speaks in his ear.*]

JEHOSHEBA

Powerful master of the heavens,
Put back the band with which you covered her eyes
When, depriving her of all the fruit of her crime,
You hid this tender victim in my bosom.   1675

JEHOIADA

Go now, wise Ishmael, lose no time about it,
Follow these crucial orders point by point;
Above all, that at her entry and on her way here,
Everything seems to her in profound calm.
You children, make ready a throne for Joash;   1680
Let him come in followed by our sacred troops.
Tell his faithful nurse to come here too,
Princess, and see that you dry your tears at once.

[*To a Levite.*]

Has passed across the threshold of the temple,   1685

You, as soon as this queen, drunk with mad pride,
And has no chance of going back again,
Make sure that immediately the warlike trumpet
Sounds to cause terror in the enemy camp.
Call all the people to the aid of their king;
Let the miracle of Joash's preservation   1690
Be noised abroad so that everyone can hear of it.
He is coming.

SCENE 4

Joash, Jehoiada, Jehosheba, troops of priests and Levites, etc.

JEHOIADA [*continues.*]

                    Holy Levites, priests of our God,
Surround this place on all sides, do not show yourselves,
And, leaving me to regulate your zeal,
Do not appear until I give the order.   1695

              [*They all hide themselves.*]

    King, I think you may be allowed to hope for this:
Come and see your enemies fall at your feet.
She whose fury pursued your infancy
Is on her way here now, and in all haste.
But have no fear. Think that, all around you,   1700
The exterminating angel stands with us.
Ascend your throne, and . . . But the door is opening.
Allow me, for a moment, to draw this veil over you.

              [*He draws a curtain.*]

You are changing colour, princess?

JEHOSHEBA

                              I must be pale,
To see the temple filling with murderers!   1705
Do you not see how numerous an escort . . .

JEHOIADA

I see the door of the holy temple shutting.
All is secure.

SCENE 5

Athaliah, Joash [hidden behind the curtain], *Jehoiada, Jehosheba,
Abner, Athaliah's attendants*

ATHALIAH [*to Jehoiada.*]

                    Ah, there you are, deceiver,
The pernicious inventor of factions and of plots,
Who put all your hopes in dissensions,   1710
The standing enemy of the supreme authorities.

You had relied on the support of your God:
Are you now disabused of your hope?
He leaves both his temple and your life in my power.
You should, on the altar where your hand sacrifices,   1715
Be ... But I must be content with the prize that is offered me.
Turn your mind now to doing as you promised.
This child, this treasure to be delivered to me,
Where are they?

JEHOIADA
                    You will be satisfied at once.
I will show you both of them at the same time.   1720

                [*The curtain is drawn back.*]

Appear, dear child, you true blood of our kings.
Do you know the heir of the holiest of our monarchs,
Queen? You know at least the marks of your dagger.
There is your king, your son, the son of Ahaziah.
People, and you, Abner, acknowledge Joash.   1725

ABNER
Heaven!

ATHALIAH [*to Jehoiada.*]
            Trickster!

JEHOIADA
                    Do you see this faithful Jewess
Whose teat, as you well know, he was then sucking?
He was saved from your fury by Jehosheba.
The temple received him and God has preserved him.
This is what I have left of David's treasures.   1730

ATHALIAH
Your deceits, traitor, will be death to this child.
Soldiers, deliver me from a hated ghost.

JEHOIADA
Soldiers of the living God, defend your king.

        [*Here, the back of the stage opens, to show the inside of
        the temple, and armed Levites emerge from all sides.*]

ATHALIAH
Where am I? O treason! O luckless queen!
I am surrounded by arms and enemies.   1735

JEHOIADA
  Useless to look round, you cannot escape,
  And God has closed upon you from all sides.
  This God you challenged has given you into our hands.
  Account for the blood you found intoxicating.

ATHALIAH
  What! So my worthless soldiers are frozen with fear?   1740
  Cowardly Abner, what trap have you led me into?

ABNER
  Queen, God is my witness . . .

ATHALIAH
                    Forget your God, traitor,
  Avenge me.

ABNER [throwing himself at Joash's feet.]
           On whom? On Joash? On my master?

ATHALIAH
  He, Joash? He, your king? You evil men,
  Consider, my armies still have you besieged.   1745
  I hear my whole camp shouting for me now.
  They are coming to my aid. Tremble, you rebels.

SCENE 6

Ishmael, Joash, Jehoiada, Athaliah, etc.

ISHMAEL [to Jehoiada.]
  My lord, the temple is clear, the enemy has gone.
  The foreigners are in flight and the Jews subdued.
  As wind disperses smoke into the air,   1750
  The voice of the Almighty has scattered this army.
  Our Levites, from above the temple doors,
  Have announced Ahaziah's son to the people,
  Have told how the child was rescued from the sword,
  And how Ahab's daughter has fallen into the trap.   1755
  At the same time the trumpet sounded everywhere;
  But its sounds and their shouts in the astonished camp
  Have spread abroad such sudden confusion and terror
  As Gideon did with the proud Midianites.
  The Tyrians, casting arms and shields aside,   1760

Have disappeared the first, by various ways.
A few desperate Jews have also fled.
But, wondering at God's manner of acting with Joash,
The rest have declared for him, at the tops of their voices.
In short, the whole people is of one mind,   1765
Women, old men, children, in joyful embraces,
Bless the Lord and him the Lord has sent.
They are all singing David's son back from the grave.
There is horror of Baal in the holy city;
The doors of his blasphemous temple have been smashed.   1770
Mattan's throat has been cut.

ATHALIAH

                    God of the Jews!
You carry the day: I admit, it is Joash;
It is vain that I try to deceive myself.
I recognize the place where my dagger struck.
I see Ahaziah in his carriage and gestures.   1775
Everything shows me again the blood I detest.
David has triumphed; only Ahab is broken.
God without pity, you only have done this.
It is you who, while I dreamed of an easy revenge,
Twenty times a day set me against myself,   1780
Now exciting remorse for what I had done to a child,
Now dazzling me with the thought of your rich treasures,
Which I feared to hand over to fire and pillage.
Let him reign then, this son, your charge, your handiwork,
And as a sign of this new power of his,   1785
Let them tell him to plunge the knife into my heart.
This is what his dying mother wishes for him:
Did I say, wishes? I flatter myself, I hope
That, unwilling to endure your yoke, tired of your law,
Faithful to Ahab's blood, which he had from me,   1790
This hateful heir of David will be seen,
Following his grandfather's ways, and like his father,
Abolishing your honours and profaning your altar,
And avenging Athaliah, Ahab, and Jezebel.

JEHOIADA

Let her be taken from the temple instantly;   1795
Let the holiness of the place not be profaned.

Go, sacred avengers of your murdered princes,
And, by her death, silence the cries of their blood.
If any be rash enough to take up her quarrel,
See that he is put to the sword with her.   1800

SCENE 7

Joash, Jehoiada, Jehosheba, Abner, etc.

JOASH

God, as you see my trouble and my affliction,
Avert far from me the queen's evil words
And do not suffer them to be fulfilled.
Allow Joash to die before he forgets you.*

JEHOIADA [*to the Levites.*]

Call the whole nation, let us show them their king: 1805
Let them come and, their hands in his, renew their homage.
King, priests, people, let us go, full of gratitude,
To reaffirm Jacob's covenant with God,
And, holily, ashamed because we have strayed,
Bind ourselves to him with renewed vows.   1810
Abner, resume your place beside the king.

[*To a Levite.*]

Well, has that woman been punished for her impiety?

SCENE 8

A Levite, Joash, Jehoiada, etc.

A LEVITE

The sword has cleared the horrors of her life.
Jerusalem, so long a prey to her fury,
Has finally been relieved of her odious yoke,   1815
And rejoices to see her bathed in her own blood.

JEHOIADA

By this terrible end, which her crimes deserved,
Be warned, king of the Jews, and never forget
That in heaven kings have a severe judge,
Innocence an avenger, and the orphan a father.   1820

EXPLANATORY NOTES

BRITANNICUS

p. 3 *First Preface*: In this preface, written soon after the first performance of the play on 13 December 1669, Racine is concerned above all to answer a number of criticisms apparently made by Corneille, who was present on that occasion. The older poet, jealous perhaps of his junior, seems to have been ungenerous, and Racine pitched into him with wit and vigour. This little dust-up explains the allusions here to 'a man who has taken the liberty of making any emperor who reigned only eight years, reign instead for twenty years' (Corneille, in *Heraclius*); to Corneille's *Cinna* and *Horace*: to 'an ill-intentioned old poet' Terence had had trouble with; and to 'someone who is ignorant', 'who prides himself more on a very bad piece of criticism, than we do on a rather good play'.

p. 7 *Second Preface*: This preface replaced the first in 1676 and in a number of subsequent editions. The change of tone is explained by the happier circumstances: 'The criticisms disappeared; the play has remained.' The preface contains a number of quotations from Tacitus, here given in translation.

The reader of the play needs to have in mind the situation at the beginning of the reign of Nero. The Roman Republic, which dates from the expulsion of the kings in 510 BC, had in 27 BC finally given way, after a long period of civil war and disorder, to the Empire. Augustus, the first emperor, was succeeded in turn by Tiberius (AD 14), Caligula (AD 37), Claudius (AD 41), and then Nero (AD 54). The rules of succession in the Empire were not settled, and Nero was the son, not of Claudius but of Domitius Aenobarbus and Agrippina, the daughter of the successful and popular general Germanicus. After the death of Aenobarbus, Agrippina married her uncle Claudius, and from this point of vantage she secured that Nero was adopted by Claudius in AD 50 and succeeded him four years later. Britannicus was a son of Claudius, and might therefore be considered to have been displaced by these manoeuvres.

p. 47, l. 1092 The Vestal Virgins were the priestesses who from the earliest times had the duty of taking care of the sacred fire of the goddess Vesta, and ensuring that it was never extinguished. The order, which was held in the highest honour in

Rome and lived under a severe discipline, was abolished only in the reign of Theodosius the Great (379–95 AD).

PHAEDRA

p. 75 *Preface*
Racine refers to 'another tragedy the subject of which is taken from Euripides'. *Phaedra* (1677) had been preceded by *Iphigenia* (1674).

p. 79, l. 12 Acheron, one of the rivers of the underworld. For the circumstances of Theseus' visit, see Racine's preface, p. 76.

l. 14 Icarus, with his father Daedalus, fled from Crete on artificial wings, the wax in which melted as they flew too near the sun, and so fell into the Aegean sea.

p. 80, l. 38 'The daughter of Minos and Pasiphaë' is Phaedra. Minos was a king of Crete, son of Jupiter and Europe. Pasiphaë, whom he married, fell in love with a bull and it was from this affair that the Minotaur, the fabulous half-human monster of Crete, was born.

p. 81, l. 73 The Amazons were a nation of warlike women who had no use for men except for purposes of breeding.

l. 82 Hercules was a celebrated hero to whom many remarkable adventures were attributed, and it is natural that the feats of Theseus should be compared with those of his predecessor.

l. 89 The Helen of Sparta whom Theseus carried off from her parents is the same who later became famous as the cause of the siege of Troy.

p. 87, l. 262 Ariadne saved Theseus, who had been shut up in the Cretan labyrinth and was to have been devoured by the Minotaur, by providing him with a thread which enabled him to find his way out. He afterwards abandoned her, pregnant, on the island of Naxos.

p. 91, l. 375 Minerva, the goddess produced from Jupiter's brain without a mother, became the tutelary deity of Athens. She is also known as Pallas.

p. 92, l. 492 For Pirithoüs, and the occasion of Theseus' visit to the underworld, see Racine's preface, p. 76.

l. 403 Cocytus, a river of the underworld.

p. 96, l. 529 The country of which Athens was the most important city.

p. 116, *l.* 1088 Neptune was the god of the sea; he is supposed to have
built the walls of Athens. Theseus' clearing his shores is a
reference to the occasion when he rid the road from Troezene
to Athens of bandits.

p. 118, *l.* 1177 A race 'more full of horrors', etc.: a reference to
Pasiphaë's affair with a bull (see above, note on p. 80).

p. 123, *l.* 1303 Minos, after his death, became the supreme judge in
the underworld; his judgments were shaken from an urn con-
taining the destinies of mankind.

ATHALIAH

Some particulars of the biblical background of this tragedy are given
in Racine's preface. The reader who wishes to follow the story at first
hand should turn to the Old Testament, and especially 2 Kings 11
and 2 Chronicles 22 and 23.

p. 145, *l.* 28 The 'mitre' is the headgear of the high priest. The word
is used to denote that worn by bishops in the Christian Church.
In the Vulgate, the Latin version of the Bible used by Racine, it
is used interchangeably with 'tiara' for that worn by the high
priest.

p. 148, *l.* 113 Ahab 'did evil in the sight of the Lord above all that
were before him' (1 Kings 16:30). He unjustly seized a vineyard belonging to Naboth, against whom Jezebel his queen had
raised false witnesses and so procured his death. The story,
with Elijah's prophetic denunciations of Ahab and Jezebel
will be found in 1 Kings 21.

l. 120 'The whole troop of lying prophets confounded' and
'flames from heaven called down upon the altar' refer to
Elijah's miracles recorded in 2 Kings 1.

l. 124 'The dead brought back when Elisha spoke' refers to the
raising of the Shunammite's son (2 Kings 4).

l. 129 The 'honours so promised to David': the promises to the
line of David are an essential thread in Old Testament history,
and to the plot of *Athaliah*. 'I will establish the throne of his
kingdom for ever' (2 Samuel 7:13). The prophecy is a recurrent
biblical theme, and in the New Testament it is seen as having
foreshadowed the birth of Jesus, 'Jesus Christ, the son of
David', Matthew 1:1.

p. 151, *l.* 232 Joram, king of Israel, was the husband of Athaliah, who
is a widow at the time of the action of the play.

p. 155, l. 334 'Mount Sinai' and 'that for ever great and famous day': this is a reference to the delivery of the Ten Commandments to Moses (Exodus 20).

p. 158, l. 404 'Moses appeared less terrifying to Pharaoh'—when the latter finally released the Israelites from their bondage in Egypt (see Exodus 12).

p. 172, l. 765 'You grow up as sweet Samuel grew'. The story of the infant Samuel, who was like Joash—but in very different circumstances—brought up in the temple, is told in 1 Samuel 1–3.

p. 181, l. 1038 'God will settle you with the rest of your perjured race'. Abiram, Dathan, Doeg, and Achitophel (cf. 2 Samuel 17, etc.).

p. 182, l. 1068 For 'Jehu' see Racine's preface, p. 140.

p. 185, l. 1144 Jehoiada here speaks as a prophet, and less explicitly than in his ordinary discourse. 'How is pure gold changed into common lead?' is a reference to Joash himself, who towards the end of his reign, and after the death of Jehoiada, killed Zechariah (see 2 Chronicles 24:20–2) who had apparently succeeded his father as high priest and who is 'the pontiff slain in this holy place'. These events, occurring long after the action of the play, have no direct relevance to the plot, but for those acquainted with later history they add a profound undertone to it. For Joash, here an innocent child, in time forsook the God of his fathers and 'served groves and idols' (2 Chronicles 24:18).

l. 1150 'Where do you lead these women and these children?' refers to the captivity in Babylon. (Cf. 2 Kings 25.)

l. 1155 'I grieve for you, Jerusalem'. A prophecy of the destruction of Jerusalem.

l. 1161 The 'new Jerusalem' is the Christian Church, which was thrown open to the 'Children she (i.e. the old Jerusalem) did not carry in her womb', that is to say non-Jews, the Gentiles, in other words, the whole world.

p. 189, l. 1264 'Jephtha's daughter' was sacrificed by her father (Judges 11:30–9).

p. 193, l. 1359 'The successor of Aaron'. Jehoiada is speaking of himself, as high priest.

p. 200, l. 1548 'So the ark, which brought down so many proud towers'. The covenant, the most sacred of the possessions housed in the temple, had been carried round the walls of

Jericho, which then fell to Joshua. (See Joshua 6.) The story of
how the Jordan was turned back to enable the people to pass is
in Joshua 3.

p. 201, l. 1597 'Cherubim'. There were 'two cherubims of olive tree,
each ten cubits high' (1 Kings 6:23).

p. 209, l. 1804   'Allow Joash to die before he forgets you.' This prayer
was not answered. See note to p. 185.

American Literature

British and Irish Literature

Children's Literature

Classics and Ancient Literature

Colonial Literature

Eastern Literature

European Literature

Gothic Literature

History

Medieval Literature

Oxford English Drama

Poetry

Philosophy

Politics

Religion

The Oxford Shakespeare

A complete list of Oxford World's Classics, including Authors in Context, Oxford English Drama, and the Oxford Shakespeare, is available in the UK from the Marketing Services Department, Oxford University Press, Great Clarendon Street, Oxford OX2 6DP, or visit the website at www.oup.com/uk/worldsclassics.

In the USA, visit www.oup.com/us/owc for a complete title list.

Oxford World's Classics are available from all good bookshops. In case of difficulty, customers in the UK should contact Oxford University Press Bookshop, 116 High Street, Oxford OX1 4BR.